PODCASTONOMICS

Unlocking the Secrets of Profitable Podcasting
FOR BEGINNERS

By

Christine Blosdale

Table of Contents

Disclaimer:

While the publisher and author have used their best efforts to be as accurate and complete as possible in preparing this document, they make no representations or warranties with respect to the accuracy or completeness of the contents and specifically disclaim any implied warranties of merchantability or fitness for a particular purpose. The advice and strategies contained herein may not be suitable for your situation. Neither the publisher nor author shall be liable for any loss of profit or any other commercial damages, including but not limited to special, incidental, consequential, or other damages.

For more information visit ChristineBlosdale.com[1]

---

1. http://www.christineblosdale.com/

DEDICATION

This book is dedicated to the fearless dreamers, those who embrace the spark of creativity within and yearn to unleash its brilliance upon the world. It is for the visionaries who strive to harness the power of their voice, crafting something extraordinary and utterly unmatched.

To each one of you, I offer this mantra: Embrace the journey, for you possess the strength, the passion, and the unwavering determination to make it happen.

YOU ARE CAPABLE, and the world eagerly awaits your unique voice.

I also dedicate this book to my mother, who told me from the moment I was born that I could do ANYTHING. Her love and support were like fresh water to a thirsty plant, giving me life and helping me grow with confidence and determination.

Thank you, maman, for everything that you have given me.

INTRODUCTION

So, you're contemplating embarking on an exhilarating journey into the Wonderful World of Podcasting. Congratulations, and get ready for an incredible adventure!

With the podcasting landscape expanding at an astounding pace, the numbers are truly remarkable. As of 2023, it's estimated that there are 3 to 4 million podcasts globally, with over 70 million episodes available in over 150 languages. This vibrant platform continues to flourish, growing exponentially with each passing day.

Are you a passionate vegan? Perhaps you're a resourceful single mom who expertly manages a $20 daily budget. Maybe you're a fierce advocate for the rights of people with disabilities or the LGBTQ+ community. Wherever your passion lies, here's the exciting news: there's an enthusiastic audience eagerly awaiting your podcast!

In fact, the latest statistics reveal that the number of podcast listeners has surpassed 465 million. These podcast enthusiasts actively seek new shows that align with their interests, and your podcast has the potential to become one of their favorites.

Podcasting presents an incredible opportunity to captivate the hearts and minds of people worldwide who crave insightful and engaging content. It's a chance to share your passion, expertise, and unique perspective while forging genuine connections with listeners across the globe.

Get ready to unleash your voice upon this ever-expanding community. Your podcast has the power to motivate, inspire, entertain, educate, and leave an indelible impact on the lives of your audience. Embrace this extraordinary medium and let your voice soar to new heights in the vast realm of audio storytelling! It is my hope that this book will also motivate and inspire you to take that leap into the world of podcasting.

What if you get stuck along the way? Just reach out to me. I have helped hundreds of people, just like you, tap into the passion and profits of podcasting, and it would be my pleasure to do the same for you. You can learn more about my private and group podcast coaching programs, plus read rave reviews and client testimonials at ChristineBlosdale.com[1].

PART I: MAKING SENSE (AND PROFITS) FROM TALKING INTO A MICROPHONE

As an International Podcasting Coach, as well as the host and producer of two successful podcasts myself ("Out of The Box With Christine Blosdale[1]" and "The 5 Minute Micro Podcast on Podcasting[2]"), with a third one on the way, I am often asked if there are easy ways to make money podcasting.

If I had a dime for every time someone asked me if they can make money with their own podcast – well, I'd be filthy rich! Here's the thing – you need to know from the get-go that it will take some time, and the process needs your serious dedication and commitment. I like to equate people wanting to create a podcast to that feeling of what it was like when you first wanted a puppy. Now, for you cat lovers out there, just think of a kitten. But for this particular example, we are going with cute and cuddly little puppies.

Sure, in the beginning, the idea of an adorable furry baby playing with you in their oh-so-adorable ways is always exciting and heartwarming. You want to show everyone your new baby. Remember how your heart melted when they would wag their little tail or when they looked up at you with those eyes filled with such trust and love?

Not many new puppy parents take the time to thoroughly think through the amount of time, money, and commitment of bringing a new family member into the household. They need proper food, consistent walks, grooming, proper medical care, and of course, love. But after the initial excitement of getting a new puppy wears off, some people will not follow the important required duties of caring for a pet.

In fact, pet adoption statistics published by the ASPCA show that each year across the United States, 6.3 million pets are surrendered to shelters. To give that some context, 17,260 animals enter a shelter daily!

---

1. https://podcasts.apple.com/us/podcast/out-of-the-box-with-christine-blosdale/id1073309606

2. https://podcasts.apple.com/au/podcast/the-5-minute-micro-podcast-on-podcasting/id1559157602

Why am I comparing puppies to podcasts? Because in the same manner people can get excited about getting a new puppy, they can also become excited about creating a podcast. Their imagination takes them to a place where they're raking in lots of money simply by sitting behind a microphone for a few minutes.

This couldn't be further from the truth. Creating a successful podcast that has the potential to bring you opportunities and profits will require time, dedication, creativity, and a massive amount of perseverance.

If you think you have what it takes to make your "Podcast puppy" happy and healthy, then continue reading, because the best is yet to come for those of you who are truly ready to jump into the wonderful world of PODCASTONOMICS!

Chapter 1: Podcasting Is STILL The New Gold Rush and Now Is The Time To Get In!

"Podcasting is a fantastic way to share your knowledge and expertise with the world, and to build a loyal and engaged audience." – **John Lee Dumas**

Did you know that the number of podcast listeners globally is predicted to reach 505 million by 2024? That's a lot of people seeking shows that resonate with their lives. And one of those podcasts could be yours!

When it comes to sheer numbers and where your listeners are located, you should also know that the US has the most in the world with a whopping 100 million active podcast listeners.

In addition to the huge success of audio podcasts that can be heard on apps like Apple Podcasts and Spotify (the two biggest podcast streaming services on the globe), video podcast production is now higher than ever with so-called "Vodcasts" reaching millions of viewers on YouTube. That's a heck of a lot of people actively seeking out content that they themselves want – and that my friend, translates into mega financial opportunities as well.

According to Market.Us the global podcasting market will exceed $234 billion by 2032 from $23.5 billion in 2023, with a compounded annual growth rate of 27.8% between 2023 and 2032. Now that's some serious money! Wouldn't you like to tap into just a piece of that?

With hundreds of different podcast genres and categories like Marketing, Business, Sports, Psychology, Finance, True Crime, Comedy, Spirituality, Relationships, etc., your options are truly endless on what type of audience you can tap into.

In other words, your potential audience is huge! With 62% of Americans having listened to a podcast (that's 205.5 million people!) when you consider the amount of global listeners there are, your potential audience increases to hundreds of millions of people.

Podcasts may be popular now, but get ready, it's going to get even bigger! And now is the time to jump in with confidence, determination and an attitude of gratitude at what can be accomplished.

Need help getting started? I'd be happy to help you map out your strategy and get you the tools you need to make the most of your podcast journey. I work with clients around the world helping them take their first steps, designing their cover art and teaching them how to record, edit and publish their masterpiece. To get your complimentary (yes, that means FREE) Podcast Strategy Session, just book a day and time that's best for you at ChatWithChristineB.com[1]. To view all of my coaching programs (along with client testimonials) visit my website at ChristineBlosdale.com[2].

---

1. http://www.ChatWithChrisitneB.com

2. http://www.christineblosdale.com/

Chapter Summary/Key Takeaways

So what did we learn in this chapter? We learned that podcasting is experiencing unprecedented global growth, making it an opportune time to dive into this thriving medium. With millions of active podcasts and an ever-expanding listener base, there's a vast audience waiting to embrace your unique voice.

The accessibility of podcasting allows anyone to become a creator, and the low barrier to entry means you can share your passion, expertise, and stories with the world. As the demand for diverse, engaging content continues to soar, now is the perfect moment to jump in and create your own podcast. Join this exciting movement, connect with a global audience, and make your mark in the vibrant world of Podcasting.

Are you ready to embark on a transformative journey and unleash your creative prowess? Creating your own podcast is an exhilarating opportunity to share your authentic voice, connect with a global audience, and leave an indelible mark on the world. Embrace the power of storytelling, as your words have the ability to inspire, entertain, and educate.

It's a chance to cultivate meaningful connections, ignite conversations, and make a lasting impact on the lives of listeners. So, seize this moment, embrace your unique perspective, and let your passion resonate through the airwaves. Get ready to captivate, empower, and transform lives with your very own podcast. The world awaits your voice!

In this next chapter, you will learn why the very concept of "sought after" media content (Podcasting) has tapped into our innate desire as human beings to consume meaningful content that is what WE PERSONALLY WANT as opposed to what has traditionally been fed to us via "programming" delivered for decades via television and radio.

Chapter 2: The Popularity of Podcasts Keeps Growing

In today's media landscape, podcasts have emerged as a powerful and influential medium, capturing the attention and loyalty of audiences worldwide. The appeal of podcasts goes beyond their captivating content; it lies in the freedom they provide for individuals to curate their preferred type of infotainment, unlike traditional programming from radio and television.

HOLLYWOOD IS PAYING ATTENTION

Even Hollywood's biggest stars recognize the immense power of podcasting and have dived into this thriving medium. Notable names such as Michelle Obama, Jonathan Van Ness (Queer Eye), Jada Pinkett, Alicia Silverstone, former NBA legend Shaquille O'Neal and even Meghan Markle has joined the podcasting revolution, further fueling its popularity and reach. Below are just a few more examples of some other big names making big profits with their own shows...

Under The Skin with Russell Brand[1]

Gwyneth Paltrow's GOOP Podcast[2]

The Oprah Winfrey Show[3] & Oprah's Super Soul[4]

The Martha Stewart Podcast[5]

Sibling Revelry with Oliver and Kate Hudson[6]

---

1. https://podcasts.apple.com/us/podcast/under-the-skin-with-russell-brand/id1212064750

2. https://podcasts.apple.com/us/podcast/the-goop-podcast/id1352546554

3. https://podcasts.apple.com/us/podcast/the-oprah-winfrey-show-the-podcast/id1499860465

4. https://podcasts.apple.com/au/podcast/oprahs-super-soul/id1264843400

5. https://podcasts.apple.com/au/podcast/the-martha-stewart-podcast/id1628369888

6. https://podcasts.apple.com/us/podcast/sibling-revelry-with-kate-hudson-and-oliver-hudson/id1485798128

Major brands, like Spotify, have also taken notice, proclaiming that podcasts will be as important to their company as streaming is for Netflix. The reasons for this growing importance are clear. Podcast audiences who subscribe to shows demonstrate remarkable loyalty and devotion, actively seeking out and consuming their favorite content on a regular basis.

ADVERTISERS ARE GOING WHERE THE PEOPLE GO

Moreover, the impact of podcast advertising cannot be underestimated. Many listeners take action in response to hearing an advertisement during their favorite podcast, recognizing the authentic and personal nature of the host's endorsement. This engagement and receptiveness create golden marketing opportunities for businesses, enabling them to connect with a highly attentive and receptive audience, all at an affordable price.

Furthermore, the shift in media consumption habits is undeniable. People are consciously reducing their time spent in front of traditional television and opting for programming they personally choose. The average listener now spends over six hours per week enjoying podcasts, immersing themselves in a wide range of topics, from educational and informational content to entertaining and thought-provoking discussions.

FREEDOM OF CHOICE

Podcasts offer a unique and unparalleled experience, granting listeners the freedom to select and indulge in content that resonates with their interests, passions, and curiosity. This freedom of choice, combined with the immersive nature of podcasting, has revolutionized the way people consume audio content, fostering a more engaged and empowered audience.

As the popularity of podcasts continues to soar, the significance of this medium becomes increasingly apparent. It not only provides a platform for creators to share their stories, knowledge, and perspectives but also empowers listeners to curate a personalized audio experience. The ability to choose preferred content, delivered by engaging hosts and experts, is a game-changer in an era where audience autonomy and diversity of voices are highly valued.

So, whether you have a story to tell, expertise to share, or a passion to explore, podcasting offers an unprecedented opportunity to connect with an ever-growing global audience who actively seeks out and appreciates the content they choose. Embrace this exciting medium, unleash your creativity, and join the podcasting revolution. Your voice matters, and the world is actually waiting to hear what you have to say!

Chapter Summary/Key Takeaways

Podcasts have emerged as a powerful and influential medium in today's media landscape, captivating audiences worldwide with their captivating content and offering individuals the freedom to curate their preferred type of content.

Moreover, the shift in media consumption habits is evident, as people are consciously opting for programming they personally choose over traditional television. With over six hours per week spent listening to podcasts on average, the engagement and immersive experience they offer have revolutionized audio content consumption.

Podcasts grant listeners the freedom to select and indulge in content that resonates with their interests, passions, and curiosity, fostering an empowered audience. As the popularity of Podcasts continues to soar, it provides an unprecedented opportunity for creators to share their stories, knowledge, and perspectives, while empowering listeners to curate a personalized audio experience.

In the next chapter, we will delve into leveraging podcasting as a powerful tool to promote and grow your business. Get ready to join the podcasting revolution, make your voice heard and even promote your business as the world eagerly awaits what you have to say!

Chapter 3: Promoting Your Own Business With A Podcast

In this chapter, we will unlock the tremendous potential of podcasting as a strategic tool to promote your business and elevate your brand to new heights. Get ready to embark on an exciting journey that will unveil a world of possibilities, where your podcast becomes a dynamic platform for growth and expansion.

Imagine the opportunities that await as you harness the power of reaching a global audience hungry for valuable content. Picture your expertise and unique insights resonating with listeners, positioning you as a trusted authority in your industry. With every episode, you have the chance to captivate, engage, and build genuine connections with your target audience.

Think of the impact you can make as you share compelling stories, industry trends, and actionable advice through your podcast. Your voice becomes a guiding light, empowering your listeners and inspiring them to take action. With every episode, you have the opportunity to nurture a community of loyal followers who eagerly await your next installment, eagerly sharing your content and spreading the word about your business.

Consider the various ways you can leverage your podcast to promote your business. From featuring interviews with industry experts and thought leaders to discussing your products and services in an authentic and engaging manner, your podcast becomes a powerful marketing tool. Additionally, the intimate nature of podcasting allows you to showcase the human side of your business, connecting on a deeper level with your audience.

Furthermore, think of the limitless possibilities for collaboration and cross-promotion that arise when you enter the podcasting sphere. Partnering with complementary businesses, influencers, or experts in your field opens doors to new audiences and expands your reach exponentially. Your podcast becomes a catalyst for valuable connections, strategic alliances, and exciting opportunities.

So, as you embark on this chapter, let your imagination run wild. Envision the ways in which podcasting can amplify your business, establish your brand, and leave a lasting impression on your listeners. Together, we will explore practical strategies, insider tips, and proven techniques to make your podcast a dynamic force for promoting your business.

Get ready to step into the spotlight, embrace the power of podcasting, and watch your business soar to new heights. The possibilities are endless, and your journey starts here!

HOW TO PROMOTE YOUR BUSINESS IN YOUR PODCAST

Podcasting can certainly enhance any business or brand by bringing knowledge of what you do to the attention of listeners from around the world. I often tell my podcast students and coaching clients that "there is always an audience for what you have to offer."

If you're a real estate agent, a coach or consultant, a healer, speaker, make-up artist or computer wizard, literally any profession or industry can have a spotlight in the world of podcasting.

Regardless of your profession or expertise, podcasting opens doors to reach your target audience, establish yourself as an authority, and showcase your unique talents and knowledge.

As a real estate agent, you can share insider tips, discuss market trends, and guide listeners through the exciting world of buying and selling properties. Coaches and consultants can leverage podcasts to offer valuable insights, share success stories, and provide actionable strategies to help their audience achieve personal and professional growth.

Healers can use podcasts to deliver guided meditations, explore alternative therapies, and inspire listeners on their journey towards wellness and self-discovery. Speakers can captivate audiences with powerful speeches, share inspiring stories, and ignite a passion for personal development.

Makeup artists can dive into the world of beauty and cosmetics, offering expert advice, product reviews, and creative tutorials. Computer wizards can demystify complex technology concepts, provide troubleshooting tips, and guide listeners through the ever-evolving digital landscape.

The beauty of podcasting lies in its versatility and inclusivity. Regardless of your profession or industry, there is a place for your unique voice and expertise. Podcasting allows you to connect with a global audience, transcend geographical boundaries, and become a go-to resource in your field.

So, whether you're a lawyer, a chef, a financial advisor, a fitness trainer, a photographer, or any other professional, podcasting offers an incredible opportunity to amplify your voice, expand your reach, and create meaningful connections with your audience. The world is eagerly awaiting your podcast, ready to tune in, learn, and be inspired by your knowledge and passion. Step into the spotlight, claim your place in the world of podcasting, and let your expertise shine.

TIPS FOR HOW YOU CAN PROMOTE YOUR BUSINESS

- Incorporate what you do into the title of your podcast. For example; "Real Estate Tips and Tricks with Samantha Stevens", pretty much tells you what the show is all about plus it promotes Samantha's name and brand as well.

- Make sure that at the beginning and end of every episode you tell listeners how they can get in touch with you for more information or to book a consultation with you. For myself, I always remind the audience that they can find out more information about me and my coaching services at ChristineBlosdale.com[1].

- Another way for you to promote your business is for you to become your very own media "Sponsor". Record and insert a 15-30 second promo/ad either in the beginning or mid point of your podcast promoting your business or any special offers you may have that the listeners would be interested in.

- Think Lead Magnets! If you'd like a way to build up your email database or newsletter subscribers you can always offer a free gift like an e-book, tip guide or course for those that sign up. Make sure to mention the easiest way for them to get your free offer by directing them to a website or landing page that will give them what you're promoting.

- In the show notes or description of your podcast make sure you include links to your website, social media and even your YouTube channel.

- If the format of your podcast is that of an interview style program invite a guest on your show that has a similar business model as yours and talk about the similarities and differences between the two. This is a great way to promote both you and your guest's business!

- If you have a service-based business (coach, consultant, advisor or mentor) you can offer a free consultation or coaching session to anyone who hears of the offer on your podcast. You never know. They could be your next paying client!

---

1. http://www.ChristineBlosdale.com

When done right, and with some clever placement on your own show, you can maximize your earning potential by letting people know how you can help them with your products or services. Just remember to not be too desperate sounding or salesy when promoting your business. People can smell a hard sales pitch a mile away and they will skedaddle if they feel they're listening to a commercial.

Chapter Summary/Key Takeaways

In summary, this chapter has provided insights on how to effectively promote your business through podcasting. Here are some key takeaways:

1. **Title Incorporation:** Incorporate your area of expertise into the podcast title to clearly communicate the focus of your show and promote your brand simultaneously.
2. **Call to Action:** Consistently remind listeners at the beginning and end of each episode how they can get in touch with you for more information or to book a consultation. Direct them to your website or preferred contact method.
3. **Self-Sponsorship:** Take advantage of the opportunity to be your own media sponsor by inserting a 30-second promotional ad at strategic points in your podcast, promoting your business and special offers.
4. **Lead Magnets:** Offer valuable incentives like e-books, tip guides, or courses to build your email database or newsletter subscribers. Direct listeners to a specific landing page or website to claim the free offer.
5. **Optimized Show Notes:** Include links to your website, social media profiles, and YouTube channel in the show notes or podcast description to provide easy access for your audience to explore more of your content.
6. **Collaboration:** Invite guests with similar business models to participate in interview-style episodes, discussing the similarities and differences between your approaches. This mutually beneficial collaboration promotes both you and your guest's businesses to a wider audience.
7. **Service-Based Promotions:** If you offer services such as coaching or consulting, utilize your podcast to offer free consultations or coaching sessions to listeners. This opportunity may lead to acquiring new paying clients.

By implementing these strategies, you can effectively promote your business within your own podcast, showcasing your expertise, attracting potential clients, and fostering connections with your audience. The power of podcasting lies in its ability to engage listeners on a personal level, providing a valuable platform to expand your reach and establish your authority in your industry.

In the next chapter, you will learn about the tremendous opportunities available for promoting your business by being a guest on podcasts. By sharing your expertise, insights, and unique perspective as a guest, you can tap into a vast network of podcast hosts and their engaged audiences.

Being a podcast guest allows you to showcase your knowledge, establish credibility, and connect with new potential customers or clients. With a wide range of podcasts covering various industries and topics, the opportunities to expand your reach, gain exposure, and attract opportunities for collaboration are abundant.

Get ready to unlock the power of podcast guesting in the upcoming chapter and elevate your business to new heights!

Chapter 4: Promote Your Business As A Podcast Guest!

It's time to break free from conventional thinking and embrace new opportunities. As the host of "Out of The Box With Christine Blosdale[1]," I know the importance of stepping outside the box of our comfort zones. If you believe that promoting your business solely revolves around having your own podcast, think again.

There is an expansive world of podcast hosts eagerly seeking fascinating guests to feature on their shows. Why not seize this chance and become that remarkable person? By investing a small amount of time in connecting with other podcasters, the rewards will undoubtedly be worthwhile.

Don't limit yourself to the confines of your own podcast. Expand your reach by appearing as a guest on other shows. This approach allows you to tap into new audiences, connect with like-minded hosts, and showcase your expertise to a broader spectrum of listeners. The collaborative power of podcasting is limitless.

So, take the leap and venture beyond your own platform. Embrace the opportunities to engage with other podcasters, share your unique insights, and amplify your presence in the podcasting community. By forging these meaningful connections, you can unlock a multitude of benefits for yourself and your business!

Finding the perfect podcast to be a guest on involves a bit of research and exploration. Here are a few examples of how you can discover suitable podcasts:

Industry Directories: Explore industry-specific podcast directories or platforms like Apple Podcasts, Spotify, or Google Podcasts. Search for podcasts relevant to your niche or area of expertise using keywords related to your business.

---

1. https://podcasts.apple.com/us/podcast/out-of-the-box-with-christine-blosdale/id1073309606

Podcast Aggregator Websites: Visit podcast aggregator websites like Podchaser, Listen Notes, or Stitcher. These platforms allow you to search for podcasts based on categories, topics, or keywords, making it easier to find shows that align with your business.

Social Media Groups and Forums: Engage with online communities and forums related to your industry or interests. Join relevant Facebook groups, LinkedIn communities, or specialized forums where podcasters and potential guests congregate. Look for opportunities shared by podcast hosts or reach out to fellow group members for podcast recommendations.

Personal Connections: Leverage your existing network and reach out to contacts in your industry who may have connections to podcast hosts. Ask for recommendations or introductions to podcasts that align with your expertise or target audience.

Guest Booking Services: Consider using guest booking services or agencies that connect podcast hosts with potential guests. These platforms streamline the process and match you with podcasts that align with your industry, interests, or expertise.

Research Guesting Opportunities: Conduct online research and explore popular podcasts within your niche. Look for shows that frequently host guests or have episodes featuring experts in your field. Study their format, topics, and audience to determine if they are a good fit for your business.

Remember, when reaching out to podcast hosts, personalize your pitch and explain how your expertise aligns with their show's audience and theme. Building genuine connections and providing value to their listeners will increase your chances of securing guest spots on relevant podcasts – and you never know – if you make a good impression, you may be asked back as a guest in the future!

Unlock the Power of Podcasts: Get Booked and Amplify Your Reach!

When it comes to pitching yourself as a guest on someone else's podcast, it's crucial to highlight the benefits you bring to the table and why they need you on their show. Maximize your impact and secure valuable publicity with these strategies:

Promote the Podcast Episode: Make a genuine commitment to promoting the episode you are featured in. Highlight the episode across your social media platforms, website, and email newsletters. By actively sharing and showcasing your appearance, you not only generate buzz for the podcast but also demonstrate your dedication as a guest.

Reciprocal Guesting: Extend an invitation to the podcast host to be a guest on your own show. This exchange offers a win-win situation, enabling both parties to leverage each other's fan base and gain exposure to new audiences. Collaborating with fellow podcasters can result in increased visibility and mutually beneficial connections.

Offer Irresistible Free Gifts: Entice listeners with a valuable free gift or bonus. Create exclusive content, such as an e-book or course and direct them to your website or provide an email address for redemption. This approach not only incentivizes engagement but also drives traffic to your platforms, expanding your reach and potential customer base.

Optimize Program Notes: Establish a requirement with the podcast host that links to your own show and website be included in the program notes of any episodes where you make guest appearances. This ensures that listeners can easily discover and explore your content after hearing you as a guest. Utilize this opportunity to drive traffic to your platforms and create a seamless connection with new potential followers.

To further enhance your guesting opportunities, consider leveraging guest booking resources like PodcastGuests.com[2] and Matchmaker.FM[3]. These

---

2. http://www.PodcastGuests.com

3. https://www.matchmaker.fm/

platforms connect hosts with potential guests and provide a streamlined approach to securing guest spots on relevant podcasts.

By implementing these strategies you can maximize your visibility, reach new audiences, and leverage the power of podcasting to expand your influence and grow your business. Get ready to amplify your presence and harness the potential of being a sought-after guest on podcasts across various platforms.

Chapter Summary/Key Takeaways

In this chapter, we explored the tremendous opportunity Podcasting presents for you to become a remarkable guest on other shows. By investing a small amount of time in connecting with fellow podcasters, you can tap into new audiences, forge valuable connections, and showcase your expertise to a broader spectrum of listeners. The collaborative power of podcasting knows no bounds, and it's time to venture beyond the confines of your own platform.

Key Takeaways:

Embrace the Guest Role: Don't limit yourself to hosting your own podcast; take advantage of the opportunity to appear as a guest on other shows. This expands your reach and allows you to tap into new audiences.

Connect with Like-Minded Hosts: Engage with other podcasters and build meaningful connections within the podcasting community. Seek out shows that align with your interests and expertise to amplify your presence and reach.

Showcase Your Expertise: Being a guest on other podcasts provides a platform to share your unique insights, experiences, and knowledge with a wider audience. Use this opportunity to position yourself as an authority in your field and establish credibility.

Research and Explore: Finding the perfect podcast to be a guest on requires research and exploration. Utilize industry directories, podcast aggregator websites, social media groups, and personal connections to discover shows that align with your expertise and target audience.

Personalize Your Pitch: When reaching out to podcast hosts, tailor your pitch to showcase the value you can bring to their show and audience. Highlight how your expertise aligns with their topics and why you would be an engaging guest.

By venturing beyond your own platform and embracing the guest role, you can tap into new audiences, connect with like-minded hosts, and showcase your expertise to a wider listener base.

The world of podcasting is filled with opportunities to expand your reach and unlock a multitude of benefits for yourself and your business. It's time to take the leap and become an outstanding guest in the thriving podcasting community.

32

Chapter 5: Establishing Your "Expert Authority"

Much like Influencers on Instagram and TikTok, Podcasters are quickly emerging as the modern world's rockstars, captivating thousands of new fans each and every day. The power of podcasting goes beyond the microphone, opening doors to exciting speaking opportunities at prominent media events, marketing bootcamps, and industry seminars.

In this chapter, we will explore how both podcasting and public speaking can be confidence boosters and are powerful tools for promoting your personal brand and expertise. If you are thinking of creating a podcast or have started one already it's time for you to take center stage, claim your Expert Authority and make a lasting impact!

Highlight Your Expertise: On your website, clearly list the different areas of expertise you can speak on in your podcast. Are you a marketing guru, a master of publicity, or an inspirational storyteller? Let people know about your unique strengths and the valuable insights you can offer. This builds credibility and attracts opportunities aligned with your expertise.

Amplify Your Availability: Make it clear on your podcast and website that you are available for speaking gigs. Showcase your passion for sharing your expertise and make it easy for potential event organizers to find and reach out to you.

Harness the Power of Public Speaking: The more you speak in public, the more people will get to know you and your podcast. Public speaking provides a platform to showcase your knowledge, connect with your audience, and solidify your position as an expert authority. It's an invaluable opportunity to leave a lasting impression and expand your influence.

Remember that speaking opportunities exist in every niche. Explore local and global events through platforms like Eventbrite. Research conferences, expos, and industry-specific gatherings. Reach out directly to event producers or coordinators, showcasing your Expert Authority, your podcast and expressing your interest in contributing to their event.

By utilizing podcasting as a springboard to establish your Expert Authority, you can captivate audiences both behind the mic and on the stage. Embrace the opportunities to share your unique insights, inspire others, and leave a lasting impact through the power of public speaking. It's time to become the rockstar of your niche and unleash your expertise on the world stage.

If you're having trouble finding out exactly what your actual "Expert Authority" is don't worry, I can help! In addition to being a Podcast Coach I also specialize in helping entrepreneurs claim their Expert Authority through hourly coaching sessions available at ExpertAuthorityCoach.com[1] and ChristineBlosdale.com[2].

Elevate Your Expert Authority Through Your Voice

Public speaking is a transformative experience for podcasters, offering incredible benefits such as increased confidence and the development of your authentic voice. It is a gateway to unexpected opportunities that can propel your podcasting journey to new heights.

Embrace Speaking Opportunities: Seize every chance to speak in public, regardless of whether it is a paid gig or not. Each opportunity allows you to refine your speaking skills, build confidence, and amplify your authentic voice. To boost your confidence, consider joining Toastmasters International, a non-profit organization dedicated to teaching public speaking and leadership skills through their network of clubs worldwide.

Promote Events: Publicize your commitment to speaking engagements by offering to promote the event on your podcast and social media platforms. By demonstrating your investment in the event's success, you showcase your dedication and establish a stronger connection with event organizers.

Leverage Promotional Materials: When you secure a speaking gig, provide event organizers with a professional headshot and links to your podcast and website. This enables them to promote you effectively and direct attendees to explore your content further, increasing your reach and influence.

---

1. http://www.ExpertAuthorityCoach.com

2. http://www.ChristineBlosdale.com

Monetize Non-Paid Opportunities: Even if a speaking opportunity is unpaid, explore the possibility of pitching an offer or special promotion from the stage. Prior to accepting the opportunity, clarify the specifics and ensure alignment with your goals. This allows you to leverage the speaking engagement to drive engagement, expand your audience, or promote your products or services.

Public speaking as a podcaster goes beyond building your confidence—it becomes a catalyst for your growth and success. Embrace each opportunity, fine-tune your speaking skills, and leverage your platform to share your expertise and authentic voice. By engaging with audiences beyond your podcast, you establish yourself as an authority, broaden your network, and uncover exciting new avenues for your podcasting journey.

Chapter Summary/Key Takeaways

In this chapter, we explored the dynamic combination of podcasting and public speaking, which can transform you into a rockstar of your niche. Podcast hosts, like Instagram and TikTok influencers, have the power to captivate a vast and growing fanbase. However, it doesn't end with the microphone. It opens doors to exciting speaking opportunities at media and networking events, bootcamps, and seminars.

We delved into the importance of highlighting your Expert Authority by clearly listing the areas you can speak on, building credibility, and attracting opportunities aligned with your unique strengths. Amplifying your availability for speaking gigs and interviews through your podcast and website was emphasized as a way to showcase your passion and make it easier for event organizers to connect with you.

We discussed how public speaking serves as a confidence booster, providing a platform to share your knowledge, connect with audiences, and solidify your position as an expert authority. We encouraged exploring local and global events through platforms like Eventbrite, researching conferences and industry gatherings, and reaching out directly to event organizers to express your interest in contributing.

Finally, we offered guidance to those struggling to identify their Expert Authority, highlighting the variety of coaching services available at ExpertAuthorityCoach.com[1] and ChristineBlosdale.com.[2]

In the next chapter, we will suggest that Podcasting presents a unique and exciting opportunity for individuals to connect with their favorite authors, celebrities, and influential figures. Unlike other forms of media, podcasts provide an intimate and personal experience, allowing listeners to feel a genuine connection with the hosts and guests.

---

1. http://www.ExpertAuthorityCoach.com

2. http://www.ChristineBlosdale.com

Podcasting bridges the gap between fans and these notable individuals, creating a space for inspiration, knowledge, and connection that is unparalleled in other media platforms. Plus, as the host, you will get the opportunity to meet some very interesting people who you have wanted to have a conversation with for a very long time! It's another Win Win Win!

Chapter 6: Use Your Podcast To Meet Notable Authors, Creators and Dream Guests!

If you're at all concerned about finding extra special guests for your podcast – don't be! You'd be surprised at who would love to be featured and promoted on your show. Especially if they have something they want to promote like a book, movie or special event.

Over the years I've interviewed hundreds of fascinating people including Roseanne Barr, Ed Asner, Marianne Williamson, Kelly Carlin (George Carlin's daughter), Mrs. Kasha Davis from RuPaul's Drag Race and Ralph Nader just to name a few. With a bit of clever investigating the possibilities to land great guests are endless.

Below are some quick tips on how to land amazing interviews with just a bit of effort...

Take a look at the titles on the New York Times Bestseller List[1] or Amazon's Top Bestseller Books List[2]. If the topic is of interest to you then you can view the author's biography and if one strikes you as a great potential guest you can reach out to them. If you cannot reach the author directly via their own website then you could try contacting the publisher or their publicity department to ask for an interview. You never know until you ask, and you never know what can happen!

Contact publishers of your favorite authors and ask to be put on their press list. You may want to do this after you have a few episodes up so they can see that you are legit, but this has worked for me in the past. They will send you out publicity info when they're about to release a new book – and this helps you get in early to score that interview!

Most celebrities will have a publicist handling their engagements. Just be professional and ask them if the person of interest would like to be on your

---

1. https://www.nytimes.com/books/best-sellers/

2. https://www.amazon.com.au/gp/bestsellers/books/ref=zg_bs_nav_0

show to promote something near and dear to their heart like a charity or organization.

Booking notable guests like celebrities, comics, and authors can significantly enhance the appeal and reach of your podcast. Here are some effective strategies to help you find and secure these high-profile guests for your show:

Leverage Personal Connections: Utilize your existing network and personal connections to reach out to celebrities, comics, entertainers and authors. Leverage mutual acquaintances, friends, or colleagues who may have connections or can make introductions on your behalf. Personal recommendations can significantly increase your chances of booking high-profile guests.

Engage with Social Media: Actively engage with the target personalities on social media platforms. Interact with their content, leave thoughtful comments, and share their work. Building a rapport and demonstrating your genuine interest can grab their attention and increase the likelihood of them considering your podcast as a guest opportunity.

Utilize Publicists and Booking Agents: Contact the publicists or booking agents of celebrities, comics, and authors. They're responsible for managing their clients' appearances and media engagements. Introduce yourself, provide relevant information about your podcast, and express your interest in having their client as a guest. Building relationships with them can open doors to guest opportunities.

Attend Events and Conferences: Networking events, conferences, and book festivals provide excellent opportunities to connect with authors, comics, and celebrities. Attend relevant industry events and establish meaningful connections with industry professionals. Use these face-to-face interactions to pitch your podcast and express your interest in featuring them as guests.

Create a Compelling Pitch: Craft a compelling and personalized pitch when reaching out to potential guests. Clearly communicate why their expertise or story aligns with your podcast's mission and audience. Emphasize the value they can provide to your listeners and highlight how the interview will be engaging and beneficial for them.

Remember, persistence and professionalism are key when reaching out to high-profile guests. Be respectful of their time and commitments, and always follow up in a timely manner. Building relationships takes time, so remain patient and persistent in your pursuit.

By employing these strategies and maintaining a professional approach, you can increase your chances of booking celebrities, comics, and authors for your podcast. These notable guests can bring fresh perspectives, attract new listeners, and elevate the overall quality and appeal of your show.

Chapter 7: Use Your Podcast To Inspire and Motivate Your Audience

In this chapter, we will explore how you can use your podcast to inspire and motivate listeners, tapping into the potential of reaching millions of like-minded individuals who share your passions. This is your opportunity to not only connect with your audience but also inspire and empower them along their own journeys.

Passion for Helping Others: If you have a passion for making a difference in the world, why not dedicate episodes to topics that promote altruism? Inform your listeners about various ways they can assist the elderly, contribute to charitable causes, or volunteer at animal rescue centers. By sharing practical tips, heartwarming stories, and success stories, you can ignite a "feels-good-to-do-good" energy that inspires listeners to take action and positively impact lives.

Personal Turning Points: Life is full of transformative moments, such as surviving cancer, overcoming adversity, or achieving significant weight loss for the sake of one's well-being. Sharing these personal stories on your podcast can be incredibly impactful, inspiring, and relatable for your audience. By opening up about your own experiences, challenges, and triumphs, you provide a source of inspiration and hope for others facing similar struggles. Your authenticity and vulnerability can motivate listeners to persevere, embrace change, and unlock their full potential.

Showcasing Inspirational Guests: Invite guests to share their inspiring stories, expertise, and journeys of personal growth. By featuring those who have overcome challenges, achieved remarkable success, or made a positive impact in their fields, you provide your listeners with diverse perspectives and role models. These interviews can serve as a source of inspiration and motivation, encouraging listeners to pursue their passions, set ambitious goals, and persist in the face of obstacles.

Offering Practical Advice and Tips: Alongside storytelling and personal anecdotes, provide practical advice, strategies, and tips to empower your audience. Share actionable steps, self-improvement techniques, and mindfulness practices that can positively influence their personal and professional lives.

Whether through personal stories, guest interviews, or practical advice, your authentic voice can empower listeners to pursue their dreams, overcome challenges, and live fulfilling lives.

Below are just a few examples of what sort of content you could create in order to help motivate and inspire your audience..

Episode: "Making a Difference: Volunteering and Community Impact"

In this episode, discuss various volunteer opportunities and ways your listeners can contribute to their communities. Share heartwarming stories of individuals who have made a significant impact through volunteering, and provide practical tips on how to get involved. Inspire your audience to use their time and skills to create positive change.

Episode: "Overcoming Obstacles: Stories of Resilience and Triumph"

Feature personal stories of individuals who have faced and overcome major challenges in their lives. These stories could include surviving life-threatening illnesses, recovering from addiction, or navigating difficult life transitions. By sharing these stories of resilience, you motivate your listeners to face their own obstacles with courage and determination.

Episode: "Finding Inspiration in Transformation: Weight Loss Journeys"

Share stories of individuals who have successfully achieved significant weight loss and improved their overall well-being. Explore the physical and emotional transformations they experienced, including the challenges and triumphs along the way. Provide practical advice on adopting healthy habits and maintaining motivation, inspiring your audience to embark on their own transformative journeys.

Episode: "Unleashing Potential: Lessons from Extraordinary Achievers"

Interview accomplished individuals from diverse fields who have achieved extraordinary success. Highlight their journeys, the lessons they've learned, and the strategies they've employed to overcome obstacles and reach their goals. By showcasing these inspiring role models, you empower your listeners to believe in their own potential and strive for greatness.

Episode: "Empowering Mindset: Tools for Personal Growth"

Offer practical advice and techniques for personal growth, including mindfulness practices, goal-setting strategies, and self-improvement tips. Discuss the power of positive thinking, visualization, and affirmations, providing your audience with actionable steps to cultivate resilience, boost self-confidence, and achieve personal growth. Inspire your listeners to prioritize their well-being and pursue a fulfilling life.

By incorporating these examples into your podcast, you can inspire and motivate your audience to take action, overcome challenges, and embrace personal growth. Each episode provides a unique opportunity to share stories, insights, and practical advice that resonates with your listeners and encourages them to live their best lives.

Chapter Summary/Key Takeaways

In this chapter, we explored the incredible potential of using your podcast as a platform to inspire and motivate listeners. By sharing stories of personal triumph, offering practical advice, and featuring inspiring guests, you can create a powerful and transformative listening experience. Below are some key takeaways...

Embrace your passion for making a difference: Dedicate episodes to topics that promote altruism, encouraging listeners to get involved and positively impact lives.

Share personal turning points: Open up about your own transformative experiences, inspiring others to overcome challenges and embrace change.

Showcase inspirational guests: Invite individuals with remarkable stories, expertise, and journeys of personal growth to motivate your audience.

Offer practical advice and tips: Provide actionable steps and self-improvement techniques that empower listeners to cultivate resilience and personal growth.

Create a space for inspiration and empowerment: Use your podcast as a source of hope, encouragement, and motivation, providing a platform for personal and professional development.

Through your authentic voice and meaningful content, you have the power to inspire listeners, ignite their passions, and guide them on a journey of self-discovery. Embrace the opportunity to make a positive impact and create a podcast that uplifts and empowers your audience.

Chapter 8: Use Your Podcast To Help Others

In this chapter we will be covering one of the most powerful and rewarding aspects of having your own podcast, which is the ability to advocate for issues that are important to you – and the world.

Bringing attention to people or organizations that are doing good in the world is a wonderful use of your podcast, and your audience will appreciate you for it.

Whether it be a food sharing program or social services for those in need, the list of important philanthropic organizations that you could showcase is endless.

Podcasting offers a unique platform for podcasters to connect with their audience and make a positive impact in various ways. By leveraging their show, podcasters can amplify important messages, raise awareness, and support charitable causes.

Let's explore different ways podcasters can use their show to help others, including collaboration with non-profit organizations.

Advocacy and Awareness: Podcasters have the opportunity to address social issues, raise awareness about important causes, and advocate for change. By dedicating episodes to topics such as mental health, environmental sustainability, or social justice, podcasters can spark conversations, educate listeners, and inspire them to take action.

Partnering with Non-Profit Organizations: Collaborating with non-profit organizations provides an avenue to support their missions and amplify their impact. Podcasters can invite representatives from non-profit organizations as guests to discuss their work, share stories of impact, and inform listeners about ways they can get involved or contribute.

Fundraising and Donation Drives: Podcasters can initiate fundraising campaigns or donation drives to support non-profit organizations. Through episodes dedicated to fundraising efforts, podcasters can encourage listeners to make contributions, share information about the cause, and promote events or initiatives organized by non-profits.

Highlighting Inspirational Stories: Podcasters can feature individuals or organizations that are making a difference in their communities or globally. By sharing their stories of triumph, resilience, and acts of kindness, podcasters inspire listeners and demonstrate the power of compassion and service.

Collaborative Episodes and Cross-Promotion: Podcasters can team up with other podcasters, including those associated with non-profit organizations, for collaborative episodes. This allows for the sharing of resources, knowledge, and networks, ultimately amplifying the message and impact of both shows.

Engaging the Community: Podcasters can foster a sense of community among their listeners, encouraging them to support each other and engage in acts of kindness. Through discussions, interviews, and listener participation, podcasters can create a supportive environment that inspires listeners to make a positive difference in their own lives and communities.

By utilizing their podcasting platform, podcasters can actively contribute to a more compassionate and informed society. Whether by raising awareness, collaborating with non-profit organizations, or inspiring listeners to take action, podcasters have the power to make a lasting impact and inspire positive change in the world. Let your podcast be a force for good and help create a better tomorrow.

USING YOUR PODCAST FOR RAISING AWARENESS

Imagine if you used your weekly podcast to spotlight an organization or group of people doing wonderful things for their communities! In 52 weeks you could shine a bright light on 52 important causes that your listeners should know about.

Feeding America is a nationwide network of more than 200 food banks and food rescue organizations. https://www.feedingamerica.org

Doctors Without Borders provides medical services in war-torn regions. https://www.doctorswithoutborders.org/

Habitat For Humanity helps families build and improve places to call home. https://habitat.org/

Do Something is a global not-for-profit for young people and social change. https://www.dosomething.org/us

The Trevor Project provides crisis intervention and suicide prevention services to LGBTQ+ youth. They offer a 24/7 helpline, online chat, and other support resources. Visit their website at https://www.thetrevorproject.org/

Girls Who Code is on a mission to close the gender gap in technology and computer science. They offer coding programs, clubs, and resources to empower young girls and provide them with the skills needed for future success. Learn more at https://girlswhocode.com/.

Charity Water is dedicated to bringing clean and safe drinking water to people in developing countries, Charity: Water funds water projects and ensures that 100% of public donations go directly to the field. Explore their impactful work at https://www.charitywater.org/.

Pencils of Promise builds schools, trains teachers, and provides educational resources to children in underprivileged communities around the world. Their mission is to increase access to quality education for all. Discover more at https://pencilsofpromise.org/.[1]

Kiva is a nonprofit organization that empowers individuals through microloans. They connect lenders with borrowers, enabling individuals to start businesses, pursue education, and improve their livelihoods. Visit their website at https://www.kiva.org/[2] to learn more about their global impact.

These organizations are just a few examples of the many incredible non-profit organizations working tirelessly to make a positive difference in communities worldwide. Supporting and raising awareness for such organizations through

---

1. https://pencilsofpromise.org/

2. https://www.kiva.org/%20

your podcast can inspire your listeners to get involved and contribute to these noble causes.

Want more ideas on how to use your podcast to help others? Do a search using keywords "non-profit" or "charities" and contact those in charge of press or media at organizations that resonate with you.

Chapter 9: Create Extra Income With Your Podcast

For you folks who decided to jump ahead to this part of the book without reading the previous chapters – congratulations you sneaky go-getter you! I like your tenacity.

"How much money can I make with my podcast?" is the most commonly asked question I receive. And I get it. People all around the world are looking for ways to supplement their incomes by doing something they're interested in. And if it's something that they love – even better! With the economy being as it is today, with the cost of living rising, finding ways to bring in additional income is becoming more and more important to families who are struggling to get by.

For many of my podcast coaching clients and students, generating income from their show is a real goal they aspire to achieve. The exciting news is that podcasting offers a wide range of possible income-generating opportunities.

Let's explore some of these ideas that can turn your podcast into a profitable venture:

Advertising and Sponsorships: In the beginning, I like the idea of directly reaching out to businesses and sponsors that align with your podcast's theme or niche. These can be located in your community or they might even be friends and family at first. You can propose sponsorship opportunities depending on the size of your audience or the uniqueness of your podcast.

I also love the idea of being your own sponsor – meaning that you can easily record short 20-30 second ads and place them in the beginning of your podcast promoting your own services or products. Just don't make it sound too salesy. A gentle reminder is enough.

Here is an example of a selfie ad: "This episode is brought to you by ME! Yes me, your wise yet loveable host. Did you know you can score a whopping $500 OFF my 4 Week Podcast Coaching Program? Just head on over to HowDoICreateAPodcast.com[1] and use promo code HALFOFF at checkout to save yourself 500 bucks! That's pretty swell huh? Yes it is! And now back to the program...”

Then as your audience grows, you can partner with podcast ad networks that will connect you with advertisers looking to reach a specific target audience. Advertisers can sponsor your show, allowing you to earn revenue from pre-roll, mid-roll, or post-roll ads.

Affiliate Marketing: You can also recommend products or services relevant to your audience and earn a commission for each sale made through your unique affiliate links.

For example, if you have a podcast about cooking, you could promote kitchen gadgets, cookbooks or cooking courses and earn a percentage of the sales generated from your referrals. A great affiliate resource is Commission Junction[2], which is the world's largest and most established affiliate marketing program on the planet.

Crowdfunding: Platforms like Patreon[3] or Buy Me a Coffee[4] allow your loyal fans to support your podcast by making regular contributions or one-time donations. In return, you can offer exclusive bonus content, early access to episodes, or personalized shoutouts to your supporters.

Merchandise and Product Sales: You can also create and sell merchandise such as branded t-shirts, mugs, or stickers featuring your podcast's logo or catchphrase. Additionally, consider developing digital products, such as online courses, e-books, or premium content that listeners can purchase.

Live Events and Workshops: Organize live events, workshops, or webinars where you can share your expertise or host interactive discussions with your audience. You can make them free of charge to get attendance up or charge a fee for attendees or better yet, seek sponsorship for these events. Use programs

---

1. https://www.christineblosdale.com/create-your-podcast

2. https://www.cj.com/

3. https://www.patreon.com/en-GB

4. https://www.buymeacoffee.com/

like Zoom to create your own webinars or workshops that you promote during your show and charge a small registration fee for participants.

Premium Subscriptions: Offer a premium subscription model where subscribers gain access to exclusive episodes, bonus content, behind-the-scenes insights, or ad-free listening experiences. Platforms like Patreon or Podbean provide tools to manage and monetize your premium subscription offerings.

Speaking Engagements and Consulting: Showcase your expertise gained from podcasting by offering speaking engagements or consulting services in your field. Capitalize on the visibility and credibility you've built through your show to secure paid speaking opportunities or provide specialized consulting services.

Remember, building a successful income stream from your podcast requires consistency, audience engagement, and delivering valuable content. By combining multiple revenue streams and exploring innovative opportunities, you can turn your passion project into a profitable endeavor.

PART II: THE FUTURE OF PODCASTING (AND VODCASTING)

Now that we got the financial side out of the way, let's take a look at some other reasons why you may want to jump into podcasting – and if you're ready to go down the rabbit hole – we will also explore what the future may hold for you as a content creator.

No one can deny that as we move into this new world of AI (Artificial Intelligence), there will be groundbreaking changes and incredible opportunities for content creators. Podcasting, already a force to be reckoned with, is set to evolve and reshape the digital media landscape in ways that we could only dream of a few years ago.

INTERACTIVE AI DRIVEN CONTENT

Imagine a world where podcasts aren't just audio experiences but interactive journeys, where listeners can actively engage and participate in the content. With AI-driven technologies, personalized podcast experiences will become the norm, tailoring content to individual preferences, interests, and even moods. Listeners will no longer be passive consumers but co-creators of the content they love.

At this very moment, with YouTube and other video platforms, we already have the ability to watch our favorite podcasters share their insights, interviews, and stories in a captivating visual format, enhancing the connection between creator and audience. But in the near future AI-driven vodcasting will take on a whole new level with the concept of hyper-personalization.

Imagine a vodcast that not only delivers compelling content but also adapts to the viewer's interests, preferences, and viewing behavior in real-time. AI algorithms will analyze viewer data, from watch history to engagement patterns, to curate and recommend content tailored precisely to each individual's tastes. Whether it's suggesting related videos, providing in-video interactive elements, or offering alternate storylines based on user choices, the vodcasting experience will become an intimately customized journey for every viewer.

Beyond personalized content, AI-powered vodcasting will also enable advanced interactivity. Viewers will have the ability to actively participate in the content, shaping the direction of the narrative and influencing the outcomes. Picture a vodcast where the audience can vote on decisions made by characters, altering the plot trajectory, or even engage in real-time polls that influence the live content as it unfolds. This interactive element will not only deepen the viewer's connection to the vodcast but also create a sense of co-authorship and shared experience.

This sort of technology isn't something on the horizon. It's already here!

WHAT THE HECK IS AN INTERACTIVE MOVIE?

An interactive movie, also known as a movie game, is a unique form of entertainment that blurs the lines between traditional cinema and interactive storytelling. Unlike a traditional linear film where viewers are passive observers, an interactive movie allows the audience to actively participate in shaping the narrative and influencing the direction of the story

In an interactive movie, viewers are presented with choices or decisions at key points in the storyline. These choices are typically displayed on the screen, and the viewer must make a selection within a given time frame. The decision made by the viewer then determines the next sequence of events or the outcome of the story.

THE FUTURE OF AI AND PODCASTING/VODCASTING

There is no doubt that AI will revolutionize the way vodcasts are produced and presented. Content creators already have unprecedented access to sophisticated AI tools that streamline the editing process, making it easier to create visually stunning productions. And as AI technology evolves, there might be a future where AI-powered virtual hosts and characters take center stage, seamlessly blending into the vodcast's narrative and enhancing the storytelling experience. But will AI be able to replace a human's capability to hold a meaningful conversation based on one's memories and life experience? Personally I don't think so but with the technology advancing day by day, who knows?

AI will also open up new opportunities for content monetization. With hyper-personalized content, creators can offer premium subscription tiers that cater to individual interests. AI-powered product placements and targeted advertisements will become more relevant and less intrusive, offering a more seamless integration between content and promotional elements.

As we venture further into the future of AI-powered vodcasting, content creators will need to play a pivotal role in shaping the landscape and defining the possibilities. The possibilities are limitless, and the era of AI-driven vodcasting is beckoning creators to embrace the technological advancements and forge a path towards a new era of visual storytelling. Embrace the future, and together, let's reimagine the world of vodcasting in the age of AI!

But it's not just about content delivery. Monetization strategies will also undergo a transformation, offering creators diversified revenue streams, from premium subscriptions to branded merchandise and exclusive experiences. As podcasting evolves, so too will the ways in which creators can sustain and grow their endeavors.

In the next chapter, we will dive into the trends, technologies, and strategies that are shaping the future of podcasting. So get ready to embark on an exciting journey that will empower you to navigate the future of podcasting and vodcasting with confidence. The possibilities are boundless, and the time to position yourself as a pioneer in this transformative era is now. So, let's dive in together and uncover the thrilling opportunities that await you in the dynamic world of podcasting!

Chapter 10: Don't Forget To Have FUN!

Now matter what the future holds, one thing to remember is this... DON'T FORGET TO HAVE FUN! If you're considering creating your own Podcast or being a guest on someone else's – one thing can be said for both – they're a whole lot of fun! Yes, there can be major work involved too. However, once you feel the joy and tap into the vast amounts of creative freedom, I think you'll agree it's worth it.

Hosting your own Podcast and Vodcast opens up a world of thrilling opportunities that are not only rewarding but also loads of fun! Step into the spotlight and let your creative juices flow as you embark on a journey filled with excitement, discovery, and connection.

Talk About Your Favorite Subjects: Delve deep into the topics that ignite your passion and share your expertise with a global audience. Whether it's discussing the latest trends in technology, exploring the mysteries of the universe, or diving into pop culture, your podcast becomes the canvas where you can paint vibrant, captivating stories that resonate with your listeners. Hosting your own podcast allows you to connect with fascinating individuals from all walks of life – experts, enthusiasts, and trailblazers who share your enthusiasm.

Be a Champion for a Cause: A podcast is a powerful platform to bring attention to a cause that touches your heart. Use your voice to amplify important messages, raise awareness, and inspire positive change. Whether it's environmental sustainability, social justice, or mental health advocacy, your podcast becomes a megaphone for spreading impactful messages, connecting you with like-minded individuals who share your passion for making the world a better place.

Unleash the Entrepreneurial Spirit: With podcasting and vodcasting, there's no limit to the creative ways you can monetize your content. Explore a myriad of income streams like accepting listener donations to support your work, partnering with affiliates that align with your values, or venturing into merchandise that reflects your brand identity. Additionally, exclusive content, sponsored ads, and product placements open doors to lucrative opportunities, all while having a blast doing what you love!

Being a guest on a podcast or vodcast is an adventure in itself, offering you a front-row seat to the exhilarating world of media exposure and meaningful conversations.

Promote Your Passion: As a guest, you get to showcase your business, product, or service to a worldwide audience, shining a spotlight on your expertise and unique offerings. Sharing your story and insights on a podcast or vodcast exposes you to a diverse and engaged audience, amplifying your reach and leaving a lasting impact on potential customers and collaborators alike.

Engage in Thrilling Conversations: Imagine being invited to discuss the very things that ignite your excitement and motivation! As a guest, you'll participate in invigorating conversations that dive deep into your areas of interest, sparking engaging dialogues with like-minded hosts and fellow guests. These interactions allow you to forge valuable connections, exchange ideas, and inspire others with your passion.

So, whether you're hosting your own podcast or vodcasting or stepping into the guest spotlight, one thing is certain – podcasting and vodcasting are not only avenues for growth and success but also exhilarating journeys that allow you to embrace your passions, connect with extraordinary individuals, and have oodles of fun along the way!

Podcasting can provide endless amounts of enjoyment and satisfaction, and the journey of podcasting is bound to be an exhilarating adventure that leaves you with a sense of fulfillment and joy. Let's dive into more ways how podcasting becomes an incredible source of fun;

• Rave Reviews and Fan Love: The thrill of receiving rave reviews from your listeners and fans is unparalleled. Your podcast becomes a platform where you connect deeply with your audience, and their appreciation fuels your passion for creating even more engaging content.

● Embrace the Learning Curve: The process of learning and mastering the technical aspects of podcasting might seem daunting at first, but it's an incredibly rewarding journey. As you conquer new skills, like audio editing, recording techniques, or crafting captivating show notes, you'll experience a sense of accomplishment that comes from honing your craft and delivering top-notch content to your listeners.

● Laughter is the Best Medicine: Why not guarantee lots of fun by inviting a comedian as a guest on your show? The laughter that ensues will create an unforgettable episode. Sharing joy and humor with your audience creates lasting memories and strengthens your podcast's connection with its listeners.

● The Bonds of Friendship: Surprisingly, podcasting often brings unexpected friendships into your life. Many of your guests can become more than just interviewees; they can become your friends and allies in the world of podcasting. The camaraderie built through shared passions and mutual interests fosters a vibrant community of creators who support and uplift one another.

Once you have your podcast up and running, why not share the fun and excitement with others?

● Spread Joy Through Humorous Clips: Create short, humorous clips from your show and share them on social media platforms like TikTok, Instagram Reels, or YouTube Shorts. These snippets will not only bring a smile to your audience's faces but also act as powerful marketing tools, enticing new listeners to join the fun.

● Celebrate and Share Milestones: When you have exciting news, such as being invited to speak at an event or seminar, share it with your audience! Celebrate these milestones on air and involve your listeners in your journey. By sharing your triumphs and achievements, you not only make your podcast more personal but also build a sense of community with your devoted audience.

In conclusion, podcasting offers boundless opportunities for fun, enjoyment, and satisfaction. It becomes a playground for creativity, a platform for meaningful connections, and a source of unending joy. Whether you're laughing with comedians, celebrating with friends, or engaging with your audience, the journey of podcasting is a delightful and rewarding experience that will leave you with memories to cherish for a lifetime. So, go forth and continue spreading the joy, because in the world of podcasting, the fun never stops!

Chapter Summary/Key Takeaways

Hosting your own Podcast and Vodcast opens doors to endless opportunities for creative freedom and excitement. Delve deep into your favorite subjects, champion causes close to your heart, and unleash your entrepreneurial spirit with diversified income streams.

As a guest on a podcast or vodcast, you'll showcase your passion, engage in thrilling conversations, and forge meaningful connections. Spread the fun by sharing humorous clips on social media and celebrating exciting milestones with your audience.

Embrace the journey of podcasting, where laughter, learning, and lasting friendships await. The world of podcasting is a playground of enjoyment and fulfillment, ready for you to explore and savor!

Chapter 11: Embracing The Cool Tools of The Trade

One of the coolest aspects of podcasting is all of the amazing gadgets and gizmos that can make you sound like a million bucks and expand your reach. While you don't need to break the bank to sound like a pro, you will need to make an investment for equipment and software if you want to make an impact and leave a good impression on your audience.

The basics are relatively simple; you will need a good computer with strong Wi-Fi, a decent pair of headphones and of course, a rock solid microphone. You will also need a quality Podcast hosting service like Podbean[1] (which is my personal favorite) and if you're only wanting to create an audio podcast you'll need sound editing software like GarageBand (for Mac), Pro Tools[2] or Adobe Audition[3]. If you want to create a Vodcast I suggest recording the video through Zoom and then using an editing software like Movavi Video Editor[4] which allows you to save both an MP3 audio file and a MP4 video file. More detailed information on some of these necessities are mentioned later in this chapter.

If all this techno talk seems a bit too much for you or if you have the smallest concern about being overwhelmed by the initial set-up, fear not. I offer a personal Podcast Coaching Program that goes over everything you need to get started PLUS I will show you how to record, edit and publish your masterpiece! To learn more simply visit **HowDoICreateAPodcast.com**[5] or check out all of my coaching services at **ChristineBlosdale.com**[6].

---

1. http://podbean.com/Christine

2. https://amzn.to/2TPGLwT

3. https://amzn.to/3an4avb

4. https://www.mvvitrk.com/click?l=1676476891&offer_id=1&pid=1689

5. **http://www.HowDoICreateAPodcast.com**

6. **http://www.ChristineBlosdale.com**

What Are The Best Microphones?

Since a quality microphone is really the most important tool you will use, below are listed my Top 5 Picks for Top Mics that you might consider..

1. Shure MV7 USB/XLR Mic[7] – MY TOP CHOICE!
    The Shure MV7 combines USB and XLR connectivity, catering to podcasters who desire a seamless transition between digital and analog setups. Its hybrid dynamic microphone element captures rich and warm tones, while the touch panel controls and built-in headphone output offer convenient monitoring and easy adjustments.
2. Audio-Technica ATR2100x-USB[8] – LOW COST MIC
    The Audio-Technica ATR2100x-USB is a budget-friendly yet powerful USB microphone. Its dynamic cardioid pickup pattern minimizes background noise, making it ideal for recording in less-than-ideal environments. The microphone also comes with an XLR output, offering flexibility for future upgrades to an audio interface setup.
3. Rode NT-USB Mic[9] – GREAT PERFORMANCE
    The Rode NT-USB Mini is a compact and stylish microphone that delivers impressive sound quality. With its integrated pop filter and cardioid pickup pattern, it excels at capturing clear vocals while reducing plosives and background noise. The mic's headphone output provides real-time monitoring, and its compact size makes it a great option for portable podcasting setups.
4. Blue Yeti USB Microphone[10] – POPULAR FOR BEGINNERS
    The Blue Yeti is a popular choice for podcasters due to its outstanding audio quality and versatility. It features multiple pickup patterns, allowing you to record solo podcasts, interviews, or roundtable

7. https://amzn.to/3DuBPTm

8. https://amzn.to/3rAMysV

9. https://amzn.to/2RQxZ0j

10. https://amzn.to/3KaptE1

discussions with ease. The built-in headphone jack and volume control offer real-time monitoring, while the plug-and-play USB connectivity ensures seamless setup.

Each of these USB microphones offers excellent sound quality and ease of use, making them perfect choices for podcasters looking to elevate their audio production without breaking the bank. Whether you're a beginner or a seasoned podcaster, these mics will undoubtedly enhance your podcasting experience.

Additional Techy Tools of The Trade

Creating a podcast or vodcast involves more than just a microphone. There are several other software and technology tools that can help streamline the production process, enhance audio and video quality, and make content creation more efficient. Here are some essential tools for podcasting and vodcasting:

Audio Editing Software: Software like Audacity (free) or Adobe Audition (paid) allows you to edit, enhance, and fine-tune your podcast's audio. You can remove background noise, add effects, splice audio clips, and ensure a professional sound.

Video Editing Software: For vodcasting, video editing software like Adobe Premiere Pro (paid) or Movavi (paid) enable you to edit and polish your video content. You can add transitions, graphics, subtitles, and apply color correction to create visually engaging videos.

Recording and Remote Interview Tools: Tools like Zencastr, SquadCast, or Riverside.fm facilitate remote interviews and record each participant's audio separately. This ensures high-quality audio, even if your guests are in different locations.

Transcription Services: Transcribing your podcast episodes can be valuable for SEO and accessibility. Services like Descript, Rev or Temi can provide accurate transcriptions for your episodes.

Podcast Hosting Platforms: To distribute your podcast, you'll need a podcast hosting platform like Libsyn or Podbean. These services store and deliver your podcast episodes to podcast directories like Apple Podcasts, Spotify, and Google Podcasts.

Streaming Software: For live streaming vodcasts, software like Streamyard, Streamlabs OBS or OBS Studio (Open Broadcaster Software) enables you to produce and broadcast live video content with overlays, graphics, and scene transitions.

Graphics and Cover Art Design: Creating eye-catching graphics and episode thumbnails can be done using graphic design software like Adobe Photoshop or free alternatives like Canva.

Remote Communication and Collaboration: Tools like Zoom, Skype, or Microsoft Teams are useful for remote communication with guests, co-hosts, or interviewees, especially for planning and pre-production meetings.

Music and Sound Effects Libraries: Royalty-free music and sound effects can be found on platforms like Epidemic Sound or AudioJungle. Adding music and sound effects can enhance the overall production value of your podcast or vodcast.

SEO and Analytics Tools: Tools like Google Analytics and SEO plugins (e.g., Yoast SEO for WordPress) help optimize your podcast website and track audience metrics for data-driven decision-making.

Remember, the specific tools you choose will depend on your budget, preferences, and the complexity of your podcast or vodcast production. These tools are designed to make the process more efficient, enhance the quality of your content, and ultimately contribute to the success of your podcast or vodcast.

Chapter 12: Gain Confidence and Become a Podcasting Rockstar!

Embarking on a podcasting journey can feel daunting at first, but remember, every successful endeavor starts with a learning curve. Just like riding a bike without training wheels for the first time, it may seem challenging, but with practice and determination, you'll gain confidence and experience the liberating feeling of creative freedom.

Podcasting, a powerful platform, can take you on a transformative journey. Each new episode you create and every fan you gain will boost your confidence and amplify your influence, spreading your message worldwide. Below are some tips to gain confidence and inspire others through podcasting:

Start with "Test" Shows: Take your time and create a few initial "test" shows. Don't worry about perfection in the beginning; it's all about learning and improving. With practice, you'll soon feel like a pro.

Embrace Your Passion: Focus your shows on subjects you are genuinely passionate about. When you speak from the heart, your enthusiasm will resonate with your audience, making your podcasting journey more rewarding.

Listen to Your Voice: Many people are uncomfortable hearing their own voice, but embracing it is crucial for podcasting success. Sing in the shower or car to grow accustomed to your voice and gain confidence in your delivery.

Be Kind to Yourself: As a beginner, it's natural to be critical of your early episodes. Remember, everyone starts somewhere, and growth is part of the process. Be patient and listen with a kind heart, acknowledging your progress.

Practice Interviewing: To enhance your communication skills, practice interviewing friends and family. Their supportive feedback will boost your confidence and refine your hosting abilities.

MORE TIPS ON HOW TO GAIN CONFIDENCE

As you gain confidence, your influence will naturally increase. So, don't let intimidation hold you back. Embrace the thrill of starting something new, ride the waves of creativity, and ignite your passion for podcasting. With each episode, you'll gain momentum, expand your reach, and become a true podcasting rockstar, leaving a lasting impact on your audience and the world.

Gaining confidence is a transformative journey that extends beyond podcasting. Whether it's pursuing a new career, public speaking, or taking on a leadership role, building self-assurance requires dedication and a willingness to step outside your comfort zone. Here are some additional examples of how people can gain confidence in various aspects of life:

Public Speaking: Join a public speaking club like Toastmasters to practice delivering speeches in a supportive environment. Gradually increase the complexity of your presentations and receive constructive feedback to boost your speaking confidence.

Fitness and Wellness: Set achievable fitness goals and track your progress over time. Celebrate each milestone reached, whether it's lifting a heavier weight, running an extra mile, or mastering a new yoga pose. The physical and mental achievements will enhance your self-belief.

Creative Pursuits: Engage in creative hobbies such as painting, writing, or playing a musical instrument. Embrace the process of learning and experimenting without the pressure of perfection. As you see improvements in your skills, your creative confidence will soar.

Networking and Social Skills: Attend social events or networking gatherings and challenge yourself to strike up conversations with new people. Practice active listening and engage in meaningful discussions. Over time, your ability to connect with others will flourish.

Career Advancement: Seek out professional development opportunities to enhance your skills and knowledge. Take on new challenges at work, such as leading a project or presenting ideas to higher-ups. Each successful experience will reinforce your confidence in your abilities.

Dealing with Criticism: Embrace constructive criticism as a tool for growth rather than a personal attack. Use feedback as an opportunity to improve and refine your skills. With an open mindset, you'll become more resilient and self-assured.

Volunteering and Helping Others: Engage in volunteer work or mentorship programs. By making a positive impact on the lives of others, you'll gain a sense of fulfillment and confidence in your ability to contribute to the world.

Embracing Failure: Recognize that setbacks and failures are an inherent part of growth. Embrace them as learning opportunities and motivation to try again. By accepting that failure is part of the journey, you'll become more resilient and determined.

Self-Affirmations: Practice daily affirmations to cultivate a positive mindset. Remind yourself of your strengths, accomplishments, and potential. Positive self-talk can foster self-belief and confidence in your abilities.

Remember, gaining confidence is a continuous process. Celebrate your progress, no matter how small, and maintain a growth-oriented mindset. Embrace new challenges, seek support from friends and mentors, and persist in your efforts. With each step forward, your confidence will grow, allowing you to embrace life's opportunities with courage and enthusiasm.

Chapter Summary/Key Takeways

In this chapter, we explored the transformative journey of building confidence in the world of podcasting and beyond. Like riding a bike for the first time, podcasting may seem intimidating initially, but with practice and passion, you'll master the art of captivating storytelling.

Embrace your authentic voice, focus on subjects you love, and create "test" shows to gain experience. Over time, your confidence will soar, and your influence will spread globally, inspiring positive change. Remember, gaining confidence extends to all aspects of life; public speaking, fitness goals, and creative pursuits are opportunities for growth. Embrace challenges, celebrate progress, and unleash your inner rockstar!

Chapter 13: Seize The Opportunity To Build Community

Building a thriving community is a powerful way for podcasters to enhance their reach and impact. By collaborating with like-minded podcasters or organizations, you can foster a sense of camaraderie and support, while creating a space where your audience can connect and engage with one another.

Collaborate with Other Podcasters: Consider reaching out to fellow podcasters who share a similar mission or target audience. Join forces for cross-promotional opportunities, guest appearances, or even co-hosted episodes. Collaborations not only introduce your podcast to a wider audience but also provide fresh perspectives and diverse content that can keep your listeners engaged.

Join or Create Networking Groups: Establish or become part of networking groups where podcasters can share knowledge, experiences, and resources. Platforms like Facebook Groups or dedicated podcasting forums provide spaces for exchanging ideas, seeking advice, and forging valuable connections within the podcasting community.

Host Virtual or In-Person Events: Organize virtual meetups, webinars, or panel discussions where podcasters and listeners can come together to discuss topics of mutual interest. For in-person engagement, consider hosting networking events, live podcast recording sessions, or interactive workshops in major cities. These events allow you to connect face-to-face with your audience and strengthen the sense of community around your podcast.

Facilitate Listener Interaction: Encourage your listeners to engage with one another through comments, social media discussions, or dedicated community forums on your website. Create a safe and inclusive space where listeners can share their thoughts, experiences, and insights related to your podcast's themes.

Support a Cause: Align your podcast with a cause or charity that resonates with your audience's values. By leveraging your platform to raise awareness and funds for a meaningful cause, you can galvanize your community to take collective action and make a positive impact on the world.

Recognize and Appreciate Your Community: Acknowledge and celebrate the contributions of your listeners and supporters. Highlight listener feedback, showcase user-generated content, or hold contests that reward community engagement. Recognizing your community's efforts fosters a sense of belonging and strengthens their connection to your podcast.

Facilitate Peer Support: Encourage listeners to provide support and advice to one another within the community. Foster a culture where individuals can seek guidance from their peers, share experiences, and grow together, creating a strong support system for all members.

Remember, building a community around your podcast is a two-way street. You will need to engage authentically with your audience, respond to their feedback, and actively participate in community discussions. By nurturing a sense of belonging and shared purpose, you'll create a loyal and passionate community that not only amplifies your podcast's impact but also enriches the lives of its members. Embrace the power of community-building, and watch your podcast evolve into a transformative force that leaves a lasting impression on the lives of those you touch.

WHAT PODCASTING COULD LOOK LIKE IN THE YEAR 2030

In the year 2030, podcasting and vodcasting could very well evolve into fully immersive and interactive experiences. Listeners and viewers would no longer passively consume content but actively participate in dynamic storytelling. Advanced AI technology might be able to personalize content delivery, tailoring episodes to individual preferences and interests in real-time.

Viewers would be able to step into virtual worlds, becoming active participants in the story unfolding around them. Interviews and panel discussions could be conducted in virtual spaces, breaking down geographical barriers and fostering global collaborations.

With the rapid advancement of AI technology, by the year 2030, there could be deep-learning algorithms enabling instantaneous content translations, making podcasts and vodcasts accessible to a global audience, irrespective of language barriers.

In this futuristic landscape, podcasting and vodcasting will become a blend of storytelling and interactive experiences, connecting creators and audiences in ways never imagined before. The future is an immersive, inclusive, and interconnected world of audio and visual narratives, where the boundaries of reality and imagination merge seamlessly.

And while all of this technology may be wonderful in many respects, we still need to be aware of the negative impacts and abuse of such technology. Most importantly, we need to keep the "human" and humane elements of our society in high regard.

Chapter 14: The Possibilities Are Endless!

Once you embark on your podcasting adventure, a world of possibilities and opportunities awaits. Here's a glimpse of the many exciting avenues you can explore:

Diversify Your Portfolio: Yes, you can have more than one podcast! Extend your podcasting reach by creating additional shows in different genres or niches. Cater to diverse audiences and expand your influence in the podcasting sphere.

Collaborate with Fellow Podcasters: Trade guest spots with your favorite podcasters to tap into each other's audiences and gain new followers. Collaborative episodes offer fresh perspectives and keep your content engaging.

Maximize Your Content's Reach: Convert your podcast episodes into written blogs using audio-to-text transcription services like Descript. This boosts search engine visibility and appeals to different types of content consumers. You can also use that text for future e-books and even as modules in courses!

Inspire Others as a Speaker: Share your podcasting journey as an inspirational speaker at local events, motivating aspiring content creators and shedding light on your journey into the power of podcasting.

Expand Your Media Presence: Reach broader audiences by securing guest spots on local TV and radio stations. Showcase your expertise, discuss intriguing topics, and attract new listeners to your podcast.

Organize Podcasting Events: Collaborate with fellow podcasters to produce live events or virtual conferences. Not only will this expand your influence, but it also offers potential revenue opportunities.

Publish a Book or E-book: Transcribe a series of your episodes and curate them into a book or e-book. For instance, create a captivating publication like "20 Women CEOs Who Broke Through The Glass Ceiling" based on empowering interviews.

Forge Alliances with Successful Podcasters: Join forces with accomplished podcasters who are willing to share resources and ideas. Networking within the podcasting community opens doors to invaluable insights and potential partnerships.

Monetize Your Podcast: Explore various revenue streams like sponsorships, affiliate marketing, or offering premium content to monetize your podcast and turn your passion into a sustainable venture.

Educational Workshops and Courses: Utilize your podcasting expertise to develop workshops or online courses. Share your knowledge with aspiring podcasters and help them kickstart their own successful journeys. For example, I offer a 4 Week Podcast Training Course[1] as well as LIVE webinars as workshops!

Crowdfunding and Patronage: Engage your dedicated listeners through crowdfunding platforms or patronage programs, offering exclusive perks or behind-the-scenes content as rewards.

Remember, podcasting is not just a medium for content creation—it's a gateway to endless opportunities. As you embrace these possibilities, your podcasting journey can lead to personal growth, meaningful connections, and a substantial impact on the lives of your audience and fellow content creators. So, unleash your creativity, take risks, and explore the vast potential that podcasting offers!

---

1. http://www.HowDoICreateAPodcast.com

Chapter 15: Some Serious thoughts BEFORE You Begin

If you've made it this far, I am guessing that you are pretty keen to start creating your podcast. But before you start, I think it's wise to really dive into the WHYS. Why do you want a podcast show? Is it because everybody else is doing it? Is it because millions of people from around the world are tuning in to podcasts? Or is it because you think it would be damn good fun and why not give it a go?

It's extremely important to know why you're creating a podcast show. If you're thinking about it, if you're contemplating the idea of creating your own show, I think it's a brilliant idea. But if you don't have the time, energy and fortitude, really, to create your own podcast show, you might want to rethink what you're doing.

Your "WHY" matters profoundly. It's the driving force that will propel you forward during the challenging times, when recording and editing episodes might feel overwhelming. Your purpose will be your compass when you're contemplating giving up or pushing through to create something truly remarkable.

Podcasting is indeed a brilliant idea, but it's also a commitment. It requires dedication, consistent effort, and a genuine passion for your topic. Before diving in, ask yourself if you have the time, energy, and fortitude to give it your all. Are you prepared to weather the uncertainties, embrace the learning curve, and keep going, even when it feels like you're talking into an abyss?

When you know your WHY, you can be intentional with your content, target the right audience, and craft a meaningful podcast that resonates deeply with your listeners. Your passion and authenticity will shine through your voice, making your show unique and engaging.

So, take the time to explore your motivations. Dig deep into what sparks your curiosity, fuels your soul, and aligns with your values. Whether it's to share your expertise, tell captivating stories, or inspire others, your WHY will be the heartbeat of your podcast.

Remember, podcasting can be an incredible journey of self-discovery and impact, but it starts with knowing WHY you want to embark on this adventure. So, embrace this crucial step, and let your purpose be the guiding star in your podcasting universe. With clarity and determination, you're on the path to creating an extraordinary show that leaves a lasting mark on both you and your listeners.

Remember, it's just like owning that new puppy. You need to feed it. You need to clean it. You need to walk it. You need to love it. You really need to take care of that new puppy podcast. Because having a successful podcast means that it does take a bit of effort to not only create it but also to be consistent with your episodes.

It's really important because you're going to start to gain fans and if they don't get content from you for months and months and months, well, they're going to dry up and they're going to go away. They're going to seek other entertainment, other information, other education from people that are actually creating content on a consistent basis.

Now, I think that it's important to note that a lot of people are jumping into podcasting because they think they're going to make a lot of fast money. Can you make money with your podcast? Well, yes and no. There's the possibility for you to make a great amount of money. It's all dependent, again, on how much effort you put into it, how you use your podcast show as a business builder.

And this is something that I love teaching my clients all about - how to use your podcast show as a business builder. The way I coach beginner podcasters is so that not only do you have the audio version of your podcast, but as we see with Zoom and the technology that we have now, you can also create your podcast episodes in a video format, so you can upload it to YouTube and social media sites like LinkedIn and Facebook.

So, in my opinion, you want to create your podcast in both audio and video. That way you can reach more and more people. I could reach a few people with my audio version of the Out of The Box With Christine[1] podcast on platforms like Spotify and Apple Podcasts. But I can reach way more people if the show is on YouTube, because in the digital age of video entertainment, that's where people are seeking out entertainment and information.

Again, it comes back to the WHY. As you're getting ready to create your podcast think about the reasons why you want to reach out to an audience. Don't just do it because you think you're going to make a lot of money, because in the beginning you won't.

It may take some time for you to build that up, but if your motivating factors are, "I have this desire to share my wisdom with the world" or "I want to help people who are struggling" or "I just to make people laugh" – then I say GO FOR IT!

---

1. https://podcasts.apple.com/us/podcast/out-of-the-box-with-christine-blosdale/id1073309606

Part III: Let's Get This Podcast Party Started!

Woohoo! Are you ready to get this party started? I am so impressed that you've come this far. Now you're ready to roll up your sleeves, turn on that microphone and start your podcast journey.

But before you take off, I'd like to offer you a bit more advice. In my Podcast Coaching business,[1] I always tell my clients that the key to avoiding overwhelm and frustration is to always remember this simple acronym...KISS. That stands for Keep It Simple Silly. I try to reiterate this easy to remember phrase to each and every one of my clients who are just starting out creating their podcast for the very first time.

For some, the whole process can seem very overwhelming. For others not so much. But for those who are a bit technophobic or who are struggling to get everything done, it can be a real challenge. All of the aspects of creating a podcast; everything from nailing down the focus and genre, creating the brand, the cover art, the theme music, the length of the show, getting over nervousness about being on a microphone or being judged or criticized... it's all part of the process of creating your podcast.

Sometimes people can get overwhelmed with the process. And I want to tell you today, the most important thing you can do is to keep it simple. You may find it easier to take this process in small steps. If producing an hour long podcast every single week is just way too much for you, don't do it. If you don't have the time, you already have a job, or you have two jobs, or, or maybe you have a large family that you need to care after, whatever the circumstances, make sure that the format in which you do the show is something that you can handle.

If it's a long format show, like an hour long, or if it's a mid-range (20- 30 minutes), or if it's a short one like my 5 Minute Micro Podcast on Podcasting[2],

---

1. http://www.ChristineBlosdale.com

2. https://podcasts.apple.com/us/podcast/the-5-minute-micro-podcast-on-podcasting/id1559157602

you need to decide on how much time is best for you so you can publish the episodes on a somewhat regular basis.

Case in point; when I first started my own podcast journey, for the first year I tied myself down to creating an episode each and every week. Why? Because when I first started, in my introduction to the show I told everybody that every week they could expect mind blowing conversations on transformational wellness with master teachers and blah, blah, blah, blah. You get the idea. And boy of boy, did I get myself into trouble with that, because I had to create a show every single week.

That meant coming up with ideas for new shows, doing research, contacting potential guests, writing up the show notes, getting to know the guests, setting up a recording date, recording it, editing it, publishing it and promoting it every single damn week. And I did that for a long time. But I'm here to tell you, you can burn out quickly under that much pressure, and you can take something that you're initially so passionate about, and it can turn into a real pain in the butt.

So what I'm saying is this - You want to keep it simple in the beginning. If that means doing an episode one week and then you do another in two weeks, so be it. That's okay. You just want to have a level of consistency. Just don't put yourself in a box where you *have* to deliver something under pressure. Be it once a week or every two weeks, if you don't have the time, energy, effort, and mind space to do it – you won't do it.

So that's why we want to Keep It Simple. Some studies suggest that a whopping 75% of podcasters don't make it past ten episodes! That's the sad truth, and we don't want that to happen to you now, do we?

Another thing that will help you Keep It Simple is for you to be organized. Having an organized home always makes you feel good, right? Well, the same goes for your podcast production system.

Being organized with your podcast is vitally important. Make sure that you have organized your folders on your desktop or on an external drive. These files can tend to be quite large, especially if you have the video files of your podcast, so you may want to consider having an external drive or you can use a cloud service. I prefer an external drive myself, but the choice is yours.

When organizing your podcast, make sure to have your folders and sub folders clearly marked. For example, I have a main folder for my Out of the Box With Christine[3] podcast and then inside that main folder I have sub folders. Those are marked with the year of publication. The next sub folders feature the episode number and guest name. Within those separate folders, I have their high resolution headshot or photo, their biography and their signed guest release form. Once recorded and edited, I add the audio and video files (MP3 and MP4) of their episode to the folder as well.

This may sound like a lot but it's not really. It is simply being organized so that if I want to repurpose the content, I can easily find it all.

Let's say in a few years I want to repurpose those episodes to publish a new book or maybe to create a course. I have that ability because I have everything saved and I know exactly where it is. That is extremely important. Once again, just KEEP IT SIMPLE.

Again, if an hour podcast is too much to handle, take it to half an hour. If 30 minutes is too much, take it down to 10 minutes. You get the idea. The main thing is that you get the experience, you get the practice, and you start creating your podcast episodes.

Once you start creating your episodes you will find that it all gets easier each time you publish them. And of course, if you're having issues or if you want to get advice from someone who has not only been there, but coaches people on how to do it all, just reach out to me. You can always contact me at my website, ChristineBlosdale.com and I'd be happy to help!

Here's one more tip on how to KEEP IT SIMPLE. Contrary to popular belief, when you're first starting out, you don't need a ton of equipment. You don't need lots of high tech, expensive gizmos. But you do want to make sure you invest in just a few things to help you on your journey into Podcasting.

---

3. https://podcasts.apple.com/us/podcast/out-of-the-box-with-christine-blosdale/id1073309606

Don't go crazy. You'll want to invest in a great microphone and your computer or laptop should be working well as well as your wi-fi connection so you can record, edit and publish with ease. So yes, you will need a few essential items to ensure you can produce high-quality content to connect with your audience effectively. Here are the most important things you'll need:

Microphone: Invest in a good-quality microphone to capture clear and professional audio. USB microphones are a popular choice for beginners, as they are easy to set up and connect directly to your computer. My personal favorite is the Shure MV7[4].

Headphones: A pair of headphones will help you monitor the audio quality and ensure there are no unwanted noises or disturbances during recording. My personal favorite is the Corsair Virtuoso[5]

Recording and Editing Software: Choose recording software to capture your audio and editing software to refine your episodes. Audacity[6] is a popular and FREE option for editing, and there are other various paid options with more advanced features. Personally, because I teach my clients the importance of having both an audio and video version of their podcasts, I will record on Zoom and then edit in Movavi Video Editor[7] which exports your files into both MP3 and MP4. This is a great option for beginners who may be intimidated by technology!

Podcast Hosting: Select a podcast hosting service where you'll upload your episodes and get an RSS feed for distribution to podcast directories like Apple Podcasts, Spotify, etc. My personal favorite and the host of all of my podcasts is Podbean[8]. You can try them for FREE for 30 days[9]!

---

4. https://amzn.to/3OKYzFp

5. https://amzn.to/3OJ99MV

6. https://www.audacityteam.org/

7. https://www.mvvitrk.com/click?l=1676476891&offer_id=1&pid=1689

8. http://podbean.com/Christine

9. http://podbean.com/Christine

Last but not least, bring your passion and enthusiasm to the table. Your genuine interest in the content will resonate with your audience and keep you motivated to continue podcasting. Remember that while equipment is important, content and connection with your audience matter most. Focus on delivering value and engaging content to create a successful and enjoyable podcasting experience.

That's pretty much the essentials that you need to get started. And if you need more help on designing your podcast studio, you can always contact me at ChristineBlosdale.com[10].

---

10. http://www.ChristineBlosdale.com

Chapter 16: The Art of The Interview

In this chapter we are gettin jiggy with the art of the podcast interview. Even if you're going to be a solo podcaster with no guest appearances on your show, you still will want to read this section as it will add value to your knowledge base, so that one day, if you do decide to have guests on, you'll be able to knock it out of the park.

I've been conducting interviews for, oh my goodness, for well over 25 years. Back in the golden days of the internet when America Online was the only thing in town, I wrote an entertainment column for the media giant that allowed me to interview some of the biggest names in showbiz. After my time at AOL had ended, I continued my interviewing prowess for 20 years when I worked as an on-air host and producer for a major radio network. Then podcasting came into my life – and I've been lucky enough to have interviewed hundreds of amazing people over the past few years.

With that kind of experience under my belt I figure I can offer you some helpful tips and ideas on how you can create the perfect podcast interview.

KNOW YOUR STUFF!

First and foremost, one of the foundational principles I impart to the clients I coach is centered around the mastery of captivating interviews. These are interviews that seize the audience's attention and hold them throughout the entire show. The primary pillar of this art is acquiring in-depth knowledge about your subject. This holds particularly true when you have a guest. Taking the initiative to conduct research prior to the interview can make a world of difference.

You will want to refrain from inviting guests solely with the expectation of boosting your listenership. Instead, if you have someone you think you'd like to have on your podcast, delve into their background—visit their website, peruse their book if they have one available. You might not need to read the entire book, but a grasp of the essentials is indispensable. Equally crucial is awareness of their website URL, along with recent projects, or services they're associated with. Ideally, well before extending an invitation, ensure you provide ample room for your guest to express themselves.

Now, this may appear obvious, but it's a pitfall to be wary of: some podcasters tend to dominate the conversation. Prolonged intros and excessive chatter by you can often truncate your guest's contribution to become a mere fragment, rendering the show imbalanced. Be mindful not to fall into this trap!

Remember, your guest has generously dedicated their time amid their busy schedule to appear on your show. Hence, it's vital to ensure your audience derives value from the interaction. This could manifest as inspiration, motivation, or fresh insights. Yet, if you curtail your guest's speaking time, how can your listeners receive these gems of wisdom? I suggest that you streamline your inquiries, abbreviate your intros, and swiftly delve into the substance, allowing your guest's brilliance to shine unhindered.

SHOULD I GO LIVE OR PRE RECORD?

So, when it comes to how I roll, I gotta say, I'm all about pre-recorded episodes. This allows me the opportunity to fine-tune the show with editing. Why do I take the time to edit? Well, as human beings, we have the tendency to drop those "umms" and "uhhs" and if you have too many it can become a bother to your listeners. But not just that, it's also about tackling those awkward pauses or random background noises from my guests. And if we're talking videos, well, the visual vibe gets a total boost too. Editing takes some time, I won't lie, but here's the kicker: your audience will appreciate the time you took to polish the episode and your guests will love you for making them sound and look top-notch!

THE STAR WARS STORY ARC

Alright, let's dive into some real nitty-gritty for those aiming to rock the podcast interview game. Picture this: stories are the glue that holds people together. They're the life force of movies and the groove in music. A well-crafted story works like magic for keeping your listeners hooked. Let's take the movie Star Wars for example. That's a story powerhouse right there. It's like they spun gold with that tale, and it's still giving birth to all kinds of cool stuff, generating millions of dollars in merchandise, sequels, the whole franchise — and it's all thanks to that killer Luke Skywalker/Darth Vader story.

Now, when you're digging for those juicy stories from your guest, you'll want to do some solid research, but also allow them to freely offer up something interesting. Giving your guest the spotlight when they're telling a riveting story will serve you well. You don't need to fade out completely—just toss in a bit of silence here and there to let the audience follow along in their imagination.

IS SILENCE TRULY GOLDEN?

Oh, and speaking of silence, it's got its own charm. Those pauses when your guest gets all nostalgic? That's art, my friend. Those moments of deep thought? They're like magnets for your audience, reeling them in deeper. Embrace those quiet moments. They're like these little time capsules, carrying the energy of something truly special. Not every second has to be a soundfest. That's where your guest's realness kicks in and your audience will appreciate it as well!

HOW TO WRAP THINGS UP LIKE A CHAMP!

Want to know how to close out your podcast with style? It's all about showing some love to your guest and giving them a solid shout-out. Pump up their works, projects, and gigs. And hey, why not toss your listeners a bone with some cool call to actions? You can encourage them to learn more about your guest by visiting blah-blah-blah.com. And don't forget about you! Make sure you also tell the audience how they can learn more about you or the podcast. You may even ask them to subscribe to the podcast or perhaps share the episode on their social media. Once you add in all the important stuff at the end you'll end up with a masterpiece in the art of podcast interviews.

Chapter 17: Podcast Your Way To Expert Status

Alright, this chapter is all about making you the go-to expert in your field through your podcast. Not in a pushy "buy this now" kinda way, but more in a "get to know you and trust your knowledge" kind of vibe.

It's all about unlocking your true potential as an expert in your field, utilizing the remarkable platform of podcasting. However, let's be clear from the start – this isn't about turning your podcast into a relentless sales pitch. Instead, it's a journey towards building a genuine connection with your audience, fostering trust through your expertise, and becoming that sought-after expert that people turn to for insights.

Imagine your podcast as a conversation, a space where you share your wisdom, experiences, and insights. It's not a megaphone; it's a window into your world of knowledge. When you embark on this journey, you're not just building a listener base, you're cultivating a community of believers who resonate with your expertise.

So, let's talk strategy. You might be asking yourself, "How does my podcast establish me as an authority figure?" Picture this: you're a financial advisor, a wellness guru, a tech wizard, or an artist who's mastered the art of visual storytelling. Your podcast becomes a platform where you dive deep into the topics that define your field. You dissect concepts, share trends, break down complexities, and sprinkle in those "aha!" moments. And all this isn't just tooting your own horn – it's about guiding your audience through the maze of knowledge.

Now, how does this build your Expert Authority? Let's explore. When your listeners consistently tune in, it's not just your voice they're hearing – it's your passion, your insights, and your genuine interest in empowering them. As you continue to deliver value, your audience begins to recognize your unwavering commitment to the field. It's like establishing an unwritten pact: you share, they learn, and trust naturally blossoms.

Consider a life coach who uses their podcast to explore mental health topics, share strategies, and offer uplifting stories. A real estate maven might dive into property market trends and investment strategies. A nutritionist might demystify dietary choices. Each episode breathes life into their expertise, leaving listeners with newfound knowledge and a sense of empowerment.

Remember, this isn't about showcasing your ego. It's about sharing your journey, your insights, and your expertise. It's about answering questions your audience hasn't even formulated yet. It's about being the guiding star in your niche galaxy.

But hey, it's not a one-way street. As you share, you also learn. Listener feedback, questions, and the occasional challenge shape your understanding of your field. It's a beautiful exchange – they gain knowledge, you gain insights, and together, you foster a community of growth.

In the podcasting realm, listeners are looking for authenticity. They crave relatable content. And what's more relatable than someone who knows their stuff inside out and is passionate about sharing it? You're not just another voice; you're the mentor they trust.

As you embark on this journey, remember that while you're sharing your expertise, you're also building trust, loyalty, and a sense of camaraderie. It's a bond that goes beyond the airwaves. So, grab that microphone and let your podcast be the conduit that transforms you from an expert to an authority, from a voice to a beacon of knowledge.

And as you continue crafting your podcast episodes, remember that it's not just about the words you speak – it's about the impact those words have on your listeners.

USING YOUR PODCAST AS A MARKETING TOOL

Here's a bit more on how you can use your podcast to claim your Expert Authority – and maybe even expand your income. If you're looking at securing more clients, aiming for speaking gigs, or hoping folks will dig your blogs or books, your podcast can be the golden ticket.

Here's the game plan: you're not just talking at someone, you're sharing your smarts, your insights, and your valuable know-how. It doesn't matter if you're into plumbing, tax advice, or mastering the art of stay-at-home mom life. The goal is to give your audience useful nuggets to level up their lives. Trust me, once you're the "go-to" person, those questions they're racking their brains over? They'll come your way.

If you've penned a bestseller, shout it from the podcast rooftops! For example, once in a while in an episode I'll drop the line, "Psst, did you know that my new book just reached #1 bestseller status in both the U.S. and Australia? You go you Aussies! Grab your copy of 'Your Amazing Itty Bitty Podcast Book' at IttyBittyPodcastBook.com[1]!"

A quick heads-up though: don't go full brag-mode on your degrees and awards during your show. Direct 'em to your website for that. Your podcast time is best spent delivering value, not listing credentials.

Bottom line? Your podcast is like a backstage pass to showcasing your expertise. By dishing out your smarts and adding that perfect call to action, you'll soon find yourself in demand and your credibility sky-high. It's all about letting your awesomeness shine without the hard sell.

---

1. http://www.ittybittypodcastbook.com

Chapter 18: Hot Tips For Recording In Zoom!

Alright, let's dive into the world of podcasting wizardry with a spotlight on some game-changing Zoom tips and tricks for the visual aspect of your show. Now, if you're part of my podcast coaching posse, you're probably already in on this secret: don't just settle for the audio version of your podcast—bring in the video companion.

Why? Because this isn't just about flexing your podcast muscles; it's about boosting your show's reach and making your mark on YouTube, which has billions of users. Yes, YouTube is where your podcast (aka vodcast) needs to be!

INTERESTING YOUTUBE STATS

- According to reports, over 2.7 billion people worldwide use YouTube per month.
- Technically, YouTube is the second-largest search engine, after Google.
- YouTube is the second most popular social media platform, after Instagram.
- Every day, people watch over a billion hours of video and generate billions of views.
- Most YouTube users fall in the age group of 15-35.
- More than 70% of YouTube watch time comes from mobile devices – just like podcasts!
- Music, entertainment, and education are the most popular genres on YouTube.

Think about it: this is marketing gold. When you record in Zoom and have your episodes in video format your podcast morphs into a visual billboard, allowing more eyes to land on your genius. And hey, lct's be real, listeners dig putting a face to that voice they're glued to. So, pull up a virtual chair and let's unpack the magic of Zoom!

Now, if Zoom is a foreign language to you, don't sweat it. It's like having a tech-savvy friend who's got your back. Think of it as this swiss army knife of tech tools. During the stressful moments of the pandemic, when millions of people worked from home, Zoom was the bat signal for businesses, bringing customers, clients, coaches, and consultants together on computer screens around the world.

The beautiful thing about Zoom is that you can go solo, or you can set up a recording with a guest from anywhere on the planet. Just ping them the Zoom meeting link, and boom, it's recording time.

Once your recording's a wrap, it's not just about saving it on your computer. With Zoom you can store it in their online cloud and here's the bonus: Zoom's got this sneaky trick up its sleeve. It can generate audio transcripts of your recordings. Yep, you heard me right. These transcripts are like gold for your SEO game and they come handy in more ways than you'd think.

Oh, but wait, there's more! Zoom's brought its A-game with a unique filter that's practically an instant makeover. I use it ALL of the time! Their "touch up my appearance" filter gives me that smooth, blemish-free glow.

Wanna know where to find this secret sauce? Head to your settings in Zoom, tap on video, and check the box marked "touch up my appearance" – then use the slider to adjust your fabulous new look. Trust me, it's like having your personal glam squad that will have you looking fresher, younger, and all-around amazing without breaking a sweat. If you're considering posting your vodcast on YouTube (and you should be!), this is your secret weapon.

Remember, if you've got a podcast, the video component is your golden ticket to greater exposure and an expanding audience. So, log on to Zoom, hit that record button, and let your podcast video shine bright like a diamond!

Chapter 19: How To Avoid Overwhelm and Burnout

Let's be honest here. For some, the podcasting landscape can be quite challenging, and many podcasters struggle to maintain consistent content creation over time. Here are some key points I feel need to be made:

Podfade: "Podfade" is a term used to describe the phenomenon where podcasters stop producing new episodes and eventually abandon their podcasts altogether. It is estimated that a significant percentage of podcasts suffer from podfade.

Low Episode Count: A considerable portion of podcasts have a small number of episodes. Many podcasters start enthusiastically but may find it difficult to sustain their efforts due to various reasons, such as time constraints, lack of growth, or inability to monetize effectively.

Apple Podcasts Directory: Around half of the podcasts listed on the Apple Podcasts directory had not released new episodes in the year leading up to the data analysis. This suggests that a large number of podcasts may be inactive.

Drop-Off Rate: Some studies suggest that approximately 75% of podcasters don't make it past ten episodes.

It's important to note that the podcasting landscape is constantly evolving, but the success and longevity of a podcast depend on various factors, including content quality, consistency, audience engagement, marketing efforts, and the dedication of the podcaster.

While these statistics may seem discouraging, they also present an opportunity for dedicated podcasters to stand out by consistently producing high-quality content, engaging with their audience, and persevering through the initial challenges. Building a successful podcast requires time, effort, and a commitment to the craft.

A CLOSER LOOK AT BURNOUT AND OVERWHELM

Okay, so let's dive in a bit further into the battle against burnout and overwhelm. As a podcaster, you're a content creator, a storyteller, and a showrunner, all rolled into one. And while the journey is exhilarating, it's no secret that the demands of maintaining a consistent podcast presence can sometimes lead to exhaustion.

Passion fuels podcasting, but it can also be the breeding ground for burnout. As you pour your heart and soul into every episode, there's a fine line between enthusiasm and exhaustion. The symptoms of burnout are sneaky: creeping fatigue, creative blocks, and a nagging sense that your podcast, once a source of joy, is now a heavy burden. So, how can you safeguard your passion from turning into burnout's prey?

Setting Realistic Expectations: The Power of Boundaries

Podcasting is like tending a garden – it needs nurturing, but overexertion can wilt even the hardiest plants. Establish boundaries that respect your time, energy, and personal life. Determine a sustainable release schedule and stick to it. Remember, your audience values consistency, but they'd rather see you in it for the long haul than witness a burnout-induced podcast hiatus.

The Art of Delegation: Embrace Teamwork

You're not a one-person show, even if your podcast's spotlight shines solely on you. Consider enlisting help, whether it's co-hosts, editors, or social media managers. Delegating tasks allows you to focus on what you do best – creating compelling content. Collaboration not only eases your load but also infuses new perspectives into your podcast's fabric.

Content Planning and Batch Recording: Staying Ahead of the Game

Imagine this: you're churning out episodes in a state of flow, and suddenly, you realize you're ahead of schedule. That's the beauty of content planning and batch recording. Dedicate time to plan your episodes, outline scripts, and even record multiple episodes in one sitting. This strategy doesn't just thwart burnout; it lets you breathe and savor the creative process.

Mindful Mindset: Nurturing Your Mental Health

Podcasting's demands can take a toll on your mental health. Remember, your well-being is paramount. Incorporate mindfulness techniques into your routine – meditation, exercise, or simply stepping away from the mic to recharge. Embrace breaks without guilt; they're not a sign of weakness but rather a testament to your resilience.

Audience Connection: Your Motivational Anchor

Your audience is your compass, your guiding star. When overwhelmed, reconnect with why you started podcasting in the first place – to share stories, to educate, to entertain. Engage with your listeners; their feedback can be a potent antidote to burnout. Knowing that your content resonates and impacts lives can reignite your passion.

Adapting and Evolving: Embrace Change with Grace

Burnout often stems from stagnation. As your podcast grows, evolve alongside it. Experiment with new formats, styles, or even guest hosts. Adapting doesn't signal defeat; it showcases your resilience and willingness to embrace change. Your podcast is a living entity, and just like life, it thrives when it evolves.

The Balanced Podcasting Dance: Crafting a Sustainable Future

Avoiding burnout isn't about dodging challenges – it's about crafting a balanced podcasting experience. Remember that it's okay to pause, reassess, and realign. Seek inspiration beyond your niche, explore hobbies, and allow yourself space to breathe.

In the realm of podcasting, your journey is a marathon, not a sprint. Embrace the joy of creation, but also respect your own limits. Burnout is a sign that your commitment runs deep, but it's also a call to prioritize self-care. Podcasting isn't just about the content you create; it's about the journey you embark on. So, with a well-tuned strategy, a mindful approach, and a dose of self-compassion, you can sidestep burnout's grasp and revel in the podcasting adventure.

Chapter 20: Your Own Podcast Success Story!

Having been a host and producer of multiple podcasts[1] myself, I can confidently state that achieving "overnight success" has taken me many, many years. Nevertheless, I stand as living proof that you can effectively utilize your podcast as a lucrative marketing tool, letting the world know just how unique and valuable you are and how they can benefit from your brilliance. Much like the impact of having authored a #1 bestselling book, hosting your own podcast gives you the opportunity to further establish your expert authority.

Will your podcast make you a millionaire? I'm not here to squash your dreams of living in a villa off the coast of Italy, BUT what is more likely, is you will be able to springboard off your podcast into other ventures. Can you become a millionaire off your podcast? ABSOLUTELY! But it all depends on how much work you put into it, who you can reach and what you do with it that matters. The one thing I know to be true is you can use it to propel your business forward and establish yourself as an expert in your field.

For example, each and every episode of my podcasts is an opportunity to inform my audience on my expertise and skillset as a coach, and in the process they get to receive some golden nuggets of information, inspiration, education and motivation.

Many of my current and past clients have told me that they decided to work with me after listening to episodes of my podcast. By listening to the episodes[2] and watching the videos on my YouTube channel[3] they felt that they got to know me, and most importantly, they began to TRUST me. This aspect of them developing trust with who I am as a coach is PURE GOLD.

---

1. https://www.christineblosdale.com/podcast-1

2. https://www.christineblosdale.com/podcast-1

3. https://www.youtube.com/channel/UCNvxA0OLgDWcEY3T6VP8JTQ

Taking the momentum of connecting with my audience first through the podcast, then moving them into my coaching programs[4] as a treasured client is just one of many successful outcomes. And this can happen for you too!

I have been asked to speak at public events, to co-author books, to be a guest on news programs, radio shows and podcasts – and I have been asked to present at sold out summits and masterminds.

Have I made a million dollars yet? No. But as you can see, the color of success doesn't just come in green.

WHAT DOES SUCCESS LOOK LIKE FOR YOU?

So what does success look like for you? Is it having pride in creating something that has true value to those who receive it? Is it maintaining a healthy work-life balance? It might be leaving a lasting positive impact on your community. And yes, it may even mean making a few sales or landing a few clients. Whatever success looks like for you, here are some other possible success scenarios you may want to aspire to when it comes to your podcast;

Community Cultivation: Imagine building a tight-knit community of passionate listeners who hang on to your every word. You foster a sense of belonging, sparking discussions and interactions both online and offline. Through live events, meet and greets and social media engagement, your listeners become more than just an audience—they become a family. This success is about the deep connections you forge and the impact you make in people's lives.

Influential Insights: Your podcast becomes a go-to source for industry insights and expertise. You interview thought leaders, innovators, and experts, gradually establishing yourself as an authority in your own niche. As your credibility grows, invitations to speak at conferences and collaborate on projects appear as well. Your podcast becomes a stepping stone to establishing your personal brand and opening doors to exciting opportunities.

---

4. https://www.christineblosdale.com/coaching

Global Reach, Local Impact: Due to your commitment, your podcast gains a global audience, transcending borders and time zones, yet you remain rooted in local issues and stories. You shed light on underrepresented voices and share stories that might never have seen the spotlight otherwise. Your success lies in your ability to bridge the gap between the global and the local, fostering empathy and understanding across cultures.

In the vibrant realm of podcasting, success takes on many shapes. Whether you're raking in the bucks, fostering a podcast family, becoming an authority, pioneering creativity, or connecting the world through stories, the journey is uniquely yours. Remember, thinking outside the box isn't just a slogan —it's a ticket to your podcasting stardom!

PODCAST SUCCESS STORIES FROM A FEW OF MY CLIENTS

SUCCESS STORY #1: The Spiritual Warrior Podcast with Barbara Savin[5]

To say that I adore Barbara Savin is an understatement. I just absolutely love this lady! We met a few years ago and immediately I found her to be gentle, genuine and with a heart of pure gold. She told me she always wanted a podcast of her own focused on sharing healing energy and Reiki with the world, but she was simply too afraid to try.

She didn't know where to start or what to do, and the mere thought of using technology frightened her a bit too. Luckily, she came to me and asked to take my 4 Week Podcast and YouTube Program[6] and I am happy to report that today she is a thriving, successful podcaster (and vodcaster) who has recorded, edited and published over 85 episodes! Now some of you may say, "Well, that's alright." But when I tell you that she's 75 years young and has absolutely no intention of slowing down – you can see why she is my inspiration and she-ro.

SUCCESS STORY #2: Women Who Push The Limits with Lynn Murphy[7]

5. https://podcasts.apple.com/au/podcast/the-spiritual-warrior-coach-podcast/id1579990706

6. https://www.christineblosdale.com/create-your-podcast

7. https://podcasts.apple.com/us/podcast/women-who-push-the-limits-podcast/id1599210358

Another client who has become a dear friend of mine as well as a valued member of my Group Mastermind[8] is Lynn Murphy. Initially, she created her podcast with a bigger goal in mind; to create a community to spotlight and support Women Who Push the Limits both in life and in business. Today, she not only runs a thriving community of women on Facebook, but she has also conducted over 50 in-depth interviews which became the chapters in her hit book Women Who Push The Limits Presents 50 Life Lessons From Inspiring Women[9]. Lynn even featured yours truly in her book. Everything about Lynn's adventures into podcasting can be called a SUCCESS!

SUCCESS STORY #3: Rediscovering Your Passion and Purpose with Patti[10]

Patti Stueland is someone who came to me with both a passion and a purpose. So how appropriate is the name of her podcast?! Once she completed my 4 Week Podcast and YouTube Program[11], Patti began creating episodes with lightning speed and now she helps listeners rediscover their own passion and purpose when life sets up roadblocks. We had so much fun together creating the framework of her show and now she's killing it on Apple Podcasts, Spotify and even YouTube. I am super-duper proud of you Patti!

SUCCESS STORY #4: The Mommy Mentor Podcast with Erinn Kennedy-Heldt[12]

Erinn Kennedy-Heldt is another graduate client of mine who took my Podcast and YouTube Program[13] and is now on a mission fueled by passion and purpose. She's a mom of three who has professional experience with mothers and babies

---

8. https://www.christineblosdale.com/mastermindbychristine

9. https://amzn.to/3KUBWMb

10. https://podcasts.apple.com/us/podcast/rediscovering-your-passion-and-purpose-with-patti/ id1689680602

11. https://www.christineblosdale.com/create-your-podcast

12. https://podcasts.apple.com/us/podcast/the-mommy-mentor/id1703159625

13. https://www.christineblosdale.com/create-your-podcast

as a registered post-partum nurse. And with 17 years of parenting under her belt, as well as nursing, she's definitely an expert authority in her field. Now she can add "bonafide podcaster and vodcaster" to her credentials as she shares her views on life and mama-hood in her rockin new show, The Mommy Mentor Podcast!

TESTIMONIALS AND REVIEWS

The success stories that I mention above are just a few of the happy clients I have worked with over the years, and I cannot express the joy I feel in my heart when someone takes the time to let others know about my coaching style. Below are just a few of the jaw dropping testimonials and reviews I have received.

"Christine is amazing. Her wealth of knowledge, and skills have made my dreams of starting a podcast a reality. She teaches and leads in a way that does not intimidate and you actually learn how to put together your podcast yourself. I have used many other programs and products before I found Christine. I wish I had found her first! She would have saved me a lot of time, money, and frustration." – **Ilya Vita (Ventura, California)**

"My business would not be where it is today without Christine Blosdale! She is a one-in-a-million business coach and branding expert that will change your life and the trajectory of your career." – **Julia Loggins (Santa Barbara, California)**

"What a great class! Christine is brilliant and really approachable. I was blown away at how much information she shared with us. Plenty of interaction and no pressure. I highly recommend Christine Blosdale and her style of coaching! Jump right in!!!!" – **Roberta Adams (New York, NY)**

"Christine is awesome. Excellent knowledge and support through the maze of setting up a YouTube Channel @captainartistlittlemate. Very helpful. Thanks Heaps!" – **Clive Jones (New South Wales, Australia)**

To view more testimonials and reviews visit ChristineBlosdale.com/ Testimonials[14]

---

14. https://www.christineblosdale.com/testimonials

Chapter 21: Let's Get You Podcasting Today!

Below is a checklist of actions and activities you need to consider BEFORE you start your podcasting journey. Don't get hung up on the individual steps, but instead, just think about what the best course of action would be for you and your budget. And as always, if you need help figuring it all out, reach out to me at ChristineBlosdale.com[1] or HowDoICreateAPodcast.com[2]

Pre-Planning:

Podcast Concept: Clearly define the overarching theme and purpose of your podcast. What unique perspective or value will it offer to listeners?

Episode Format: Decide on the structure of your episodes – whether they'll be solo monologues, co-hosted conversations, interviews, storytelling, or a combination. Also consider the average length in minutes your podcast will be.

Episode Topics: Compile a list of engaging and relevant topics that align with your podcast's theme. This will help you plan your content in advance.

Branding: Create a compelling podcast name, design a logo, and develop cover art that visually represents your podcast's identity and appeals to your target audience.

Episode Outline: Draft outlines for your initial episodes. This will provide you with a roadmap for content flow and help maintain a structured approach.

Recording Equipment:

Microphone: Invest in a high-quality microphone[3] to ensure clear and professional audio recording, which is essential for delivering a successful listening experience.

---

1. https://www.christineblosdale.com

2. http://www.howdoicreateapodcast.com

3. https://amzn.to/45FPe7k

Headphones: Use high-quality headphones[4] to monitor your audio quality while recording. This helps identify any issues like "popping" or "smacking" and ensures optimal sound.

Recording Space: Select a quiet and well-treated recording space to minimize background noise and reverberation, resulting in cleaner recordings. For the video version of your podcast make sure the background isn't too busy or messy and that you are well lit.

Software and Tools:

Recording Device: Prepare your computer or dedicated recording device to capture high-quality audio for your episodes.

Skype/Zoom: If recording yourself on video or if you are conducting remote interviews, have either Skype or Zoom software ready to ensure smooth video recording/

File Storage: Set up an organized system for storing your podcast files, ensuring easy access and retrieval.

Recording Software: If preparing for just an audio podcast ONLY, install and become familiar with audio recording and editing software such as Audacity, Adobe Audition, or GarageBand.

Editing and Post-Production:

Editing Software: Acquaint yourself with your chosen editing software to cut, enhance, and arrange clips, creating polished and professional episodes. I prefer editing videos of my podcast recorded in Zoom in Movavi Video Editor[5] in order to get both audio and video files.

Music and Sound Effects: Source royalty-free music and sound effects to incorporate into your podcast for intros, outros, transitions, and ambiance. I personally use services like Epidemic Sound and Shutterfly.

---

4. https://amzn.to/3E9gFuH

5. https://www.mvvitrk.com/click?l=1676476891&offer_id=1&pid=1689

Editing Skills: Develop basic audio (and video) editing skills or consider outsourcing the editing process to ensure high-quality episode production. If you are absolutely terrified of the idea of editing your episodes reach out to me at ChristineBlosdale.com[6] and I will happily give you a quote.

Hosting and Distribution:

Podcast Hosting Platform: Select a podcast hosting service to store and distribute your episodes to podcast directories. Personally, due to their reliable service as well as cost I use and recommend to my clients Podbean[7].

RSS Feed: Your hosting platform generates an RSS feed that you'll submit to various podcast directories like Apple Podcasts or Spotify for syndication.

Distribution Platforms: Submit your podcast RSS feed to major platforms like Apple Podcasts, Spotify, Google Podcasts, etc., to expand your reach.

Promotion and Marketing:

Social Media Profiles: Establish active social media profiles for your podcast on platforms relevant to your target audience to engage and share updates.

Trailer/Intro Episode: Create a captivating trailer or intro episode that introduces your podcast and its value proposition before your official launch.

Website or Blog: Develop a dedicated website, landing page or blog to host episode show notes, transcripts, additional content, and contact information.

Promotional Material: Design visually appealing promotional graphics to use on social media and podcast directories, attracting potential listeners.

Launch Plan: Strategize your podcast launch by determining a release schedule, planning teaser campaigns, and promoting any guest appearances.

Engagement and Analytics:

---

6. http://www.christineblosdale.com/

7. http://podbean.com/Christine

Listener Interaction: Set up channels for listeners to connect with you, such as email, social media, or a website contact form, encouraging feedback and engagement.

Analytics Tools: Implement analytics tools to track podcast performance, such as download numbers, listener demographics, and engagement metrics. Podbean[8] provides these stats and more.

---

8. http://podbean.com/Christine

Chapter 22: Save Time and Money (and Your Mind) With A Podcast Coach

Embarking on a podcasting journey can be exhilarating, yet daunting for newcomers. This is where the wisdom of hiring a seasoned podcasting coach comes to light. A coach offers personalized guidance, imparting insights honed through experience. They help new podcasters define their niche, craft compelling content, and establish a consistent tone.

A coach provides hands-on training on equipment, recording techniques, and editing skills, ensuring a polished final product. Mistakes are inevitable, but a coach's constructive feedback can help accelerate growth. Additionally, a coach offers confidence, helping newcomers overcome mic fright and imposter syndrome.

A professional podcast coach will also streamline the learning curve, preventing frustration and information overload. Their mentorship fosters growth, transforming novices into confident and competent podcasters. With a coach by their side, newbie podcasters gain a supportive ally, ready to guide them through challenges and celebrate their successes, ultimately turning their podcasting dreams into reality.

Why Should You Consider Working With A Coach?

In today's digital age, where content consumption is rapidly evolving, harnessing the power of podcasts under the guidance of an experienced coach presents a golden opportunity for both individuals and businesses.

So why should you get a podcast coach? Collaborating with a seasoned expert who brings a wealth of expertise in broadcasting and communication is simply priceless. This takes out the frustration and delays of the whole process, and you get a working viable podcast in no time!

A podcast coach's guidance ensures that the podcast not only maintains a high level of professionalism but also radiates an authentic charm that resonates with listeners.

And since podcasts provide a unique channel for business promotion, with an experienced coach's direction, podcasters can strategically infuse their episodes with valuable insights related to their industry. This not only promotes their products or services, but it also expands their reach and influence.

By partnering with a skilled coach, individuals and businesses can craft a podcast that not only reflects their brand values but also propels them into the spotlight.

WANT TO GET STARTED CREATING YOUR OWN PODCAST?

If you'd like to explore the possibilities on how to use your podcast as a successful business tool I would love to have a conversation with you. I have been training clients from all around the world on how to create successful podcasts to promote their businesses and brands – and I can do the same for you!

To see all of my coaching programs visit ChristineBlosdale.com[1] or to book your complimentary strategy session visit ChatWithChristineB.com[2] and pick a day and time that is best for you. It's that simple.

ABOUT CHRISTINE BLOSDALE

Specializing in Podcasting, Radio, Branding and Multimedia, Christine Blosdale has worked with global thought leaders, elite coaches, bestselling authors and social media influencers from around the world. She's also an International #1 Amazon Bestselling Author, Award Winning Media Personality with over 25+ years experience and a featured contributor to America Online, MSN, Woman's Day, Ticker News, Pacifica Radio, Take 5 Magazine, Hollywood.com and MarketWatch. For more information visit ChristineBlosdale.com[3]

---

1. http://www.christineblosdale.com/

2. http://www.ChatWithChristineB.com

3. http://www.christineblosdale.com/